"IF YOU WANT ME TO NAME DROP"

A Diary of a West End Wendy

SCOTT ST MARTYN

COPYRIGHT

FOREWORD

The idea for this book came in a most unlikely place, a small bar in Oliva in the province of Valencia, Spain.

One day I was chatting to Elaine, the president of the local drama group. We were talking about pantomime, when I mentioned I had seen the likes of Cliff Richard, Terry Scott, and Una Stubbs in panto as a child.

Elaine smiled. "I love it when people name drop."

Strange how a few words can trigger a thought, a memory, a ghost from the past.

If I wanted to name drop, believe me, I could.

Therefore, firstly I would like to thank Elaine Hyderman for giving me the idea for writing this book. Secondly, I began a little page for twenty or so people on social media to try out my scribblings and moments of rambling. To my merry band, I thank you for your help, and especially to Lin Warner, Toby Kay and Anne Persson, for their constant encouragement and guidance.

I hope you find this book not just about my career, but also an insight into the backstage world of London's West End, and provincial theatres. Forty years is a long time to live a dream. I hope you enjoy living it with me

Scott St. Martyn
Saint Laurent D'Arce, France
February 2018

Chapter One

Please put your son on the stage, Mrs Worthington

My poor mother and father. From an early age I would be putting on plays and dressing up at every opportunity. I even staged my own carnival once, with a cast of three! It was fabulous. Well, in my eyes it was.

However, my theatrical achievements had been limited until that fateful morning Dad came home from work and announced that the local operatic society was putting on *Oliver*. They were looking for boys to play orphans. I knew I was perfect for it, having suspected for many years that I was a prince stolen away by some evil baron and placed in an orphanage; a dream that every boy has. No? Just me then.

The evening of the auditions came, and I was taken along by Dad to a school hall in West Watford. I was greeted by a buzz of excited young boys, some of whom I suspect had the same dream as me of being a stolen prince. Thinking back, some of them had advanced to dreams of captured princesses or even queens.

To my delight, I was picked as an orphan, and given a script to go away and learn a page of dialogue for a second audition to play the part of Oliver. From that moment on, our house was transformed into my own little stage school, and everyone was expected to join in. I was sent for singing lessons and was off-script days before the final casting. At the age of eleven, the dream was born, and I got the part.

In our house we lived *Oliver* for months. Amateur companies have rehearsals for months and months, but that was fine by me. Another boy called Allan shared the role with me; luckily he was and is a lovely guy. We became great friends.

I was quite shy as a child, not with my family and friends but with people I didn't know. I was permanently on my guard, as I knew I was different. I just thought it was because I liked lots of different things from the other boys; you have to remember gay had not been invented then! Being in the show allowed me to be myself. When you can sing and act at such a young age and are surrounded by people who also love theatre, you are different in another way. To others it may have just been me showing off, but to me it was being the boy I wanted to be.

It was at this time that two people came into my life. The choreographer for the production was a larger than life, beautiful woman called Sidi Scott, and it fascinated me the way she talked about her life as a professional dancer in the West End. Sidi was pure magic to me. The other was a young boy who had moved up from Kent and was now going to my school. Martyn Knight was, and still is a big part of my life and, if you haven't guessed, that is how I got my name Scott St Martyn! More about these two later.

The time had come to put the show into the theatre. The Friday before we opened was costume call. Oh, how I loved it! I made my dad take me earlier than my call so I could watch everyone dress. Having played for years with home-made puppet theatres, can you imagine my delight in playing with real live people? The best was yet to come, as for my orphan's costume I had the most beautiful gold jacket and high-waisted trousers with a hat. The rest of the weekend was a blur of band calls and scenery rehearsals leading up to the opening night when it was finally my turn. On 15th February 1969, I stood on the Palace Theatre stage in Watford and sang my heart out.

Please let me be fifteen soon

Remember as a child when you came back from holiday and had that empty feeling? That feeling that your life was over and everything was so drab around you? That's how I felt when *Oliver* had finished. What was I to do? For those few months I had been living my dream, and now I was just me again. There would always be the next show, or so I thought, but rules are rules. I couldn't join the operatic society until I was fifteen. What? That was three years I would have to wait, and in teenage years that's forever. I decided if I couldn't be in their shows, I would be in my own and at school.

The Evils of Sir Jasper Heartless. I wrote it, directed it and, yes you guessed it, I played Sir Jasper. My new best friend, Martyn Knight, was given the part of the vicar. Martyn had just moved to the area because his father had a new job, and his mother was a leading lady in the other local operatic society 'Cassio', so we had lots in common. Martyn lived in one of the nicer parts of Watford and his father was 'management'. We lived in a council house and my dad was a 'union man'. As children, I don't think we noticed how different our two families were and, as they say, opposites attract.

After the great, critically acclaimed production of *Sir Jasper* (one performance to a group of pensioners), I had some good news. I was to be in another show for Watford Operatic Society, as were my sister Linda, and my dad; both of them had good voices and, as Dad knew most of the company because he had been my chaperone in *Oliver*, I could also be in a newly created part for me, the page boy in Acts Two and Three of *The Boyfriend*. It was a non-speaking part, but this was not going to stop me from getting that round of applause.

The director was a local actor called Frank Jarvis, he was best known for being in the film *The Italian Job* with Michael Caine. The wonderful Sidi was to choreograph. I was in heaven being back in rehearsals. It's strange, because when I was doing the shows with the 'am drams', I never wanted rehearsals to finish, whereas when I went into the business as a professional, I couldn't wait to get on the stage.

My moment came in Act Two. I was to walk across the stage with a tray with a glass of champagne on it, stony faced, looking out front... just walk. The first night, I walked, got a laugh, not good enough for me. By the end of the week, it had developed into applause. That's all I wanted to hear, just the applause - the actor's drug of choice.

One night, Frank was in the wings as I made my exit. "You cheeky little sod, you are working the audience, aren't you?" I learnt that at a very early age. One of the nice points of this story is that years later, both Frank and Sidi were my referees for my Equity Card.

By the time I was fifteen, I joined both the local operatic groups as did Martyn. Then the night came that changed everything for me.

What's a Step Ball Change?

Now a veteran of musical theatre, having been in four shows: two at the Palace Theatre, Watford, *Oliver* and *The Merry Widow*, *The Boyfriend* at Watford College, and *The Pirates of Penzance* at St Michael's Hall, I decided it was time I auditioned for a principal part. After all, I was sixteen now and surely ready for local stardom?

Cassio Operatic Society were doing a production of *The Music Man*. Martyn and I auditioned for the juvenile lead, Tommy. Unfortunately, we were both unsuccessful but, to our amazement, we were cast as dancers; neither of us had ever danced before. I had wanted to go to dance classes when I was younger, but my dad wasn't keen on his son going to dance school; I could have singing lessons but not dance.

On the first evening of rehearsals, Sidi was setting the Library Ballet. She took me by the hand and moved me to my starting position.

"Now you do two step ball changes until you get to here." I looked blankly at her and all the other dancers.

"What's a step ball change?" Everyone in the room laughed. I was taken away by Liz Harrison and she proceeded to teach me my first step ball change, a step I was to use many times in the future.

For years, when the phone rang and it was Sidi, I knew it was to ask if I was free to do another show for her and, if Sidi asked, I never said no, whether it be St Albans, Abbots Langley or Harpenden. I would get a bus, train or be picked up by one of the other 'SIDS Kids' as we were known locally, and dance my evenings away. Some weeks, I would have

—

8

rehearsals every night for up to three different shows, leaving only Saturdays free. I didn't care. I loved it.

I used to think I did many years on the amateur stage. It was only five, it just felt longer because of all the shows I did in such a short period of time. After a while, I did notice one thing, work was getting in the way of shows. Something had to be done!

Plan A: Make a list and start from the top

A decision had been made. I wanted to go professional and to do that I would need to go to college. I sat down with my parents and we had a long chat, they were both very supportive.

"If that's what you want, even if I have to get another job, we will work it out." my mother said.

First thing I did, was to make a list of the colleges I wanted to try for. Number one was Arts Educational School (Arts Ed), it was where Sidi had gone and it had a course for musical theatre, then the Central School of Speech and Drama, and then RADA.

I remember Dad and I sat at the dining table and filled out the forms. It wasn't until years later, I found out that Dad was worried sick about how they were going to find the money for it all, but good news was on the horizon on that issue. I was accepted for auditions at all three academies, the first being Arts Ed.

Mum and I got a train to Euston, then Tube to the Barbican. I don't remember being nervous, well I wasn't, but Mum was a

—

mess. I was told to prepare a song, and bring dance clothes. First thing we did was a ballet class. Now, I had only ever done a few steps with Sidi, but a whole class... I felt way out of my depth. We had to be examined for good spine and hips, and after that we had to stand in front of the Board and tell them why we wanted to attend the college. I took a deep breath and pretended to be confident; thank God they couldn't hear my knees knocking! On the Board was Miss Fisher who ran the school agency, Bernard Jameson, Head of Musical Theatre or 50/50 as it was called, Eve Pettinger was Head of Ballet, and Mrs Jack, Principal of the school and college. They seemed to be impressed as I remember I made them laugh a few times.

"Now young man, what are you going to sing for us?" Miss Jack asked. I told them I was giving them 'Get me to the church on time' and the Board all sat up in anticipation. I started to sing and, to my surprise, Miss Jack joined in with me. I even got applause! I left the room having done my best; that was on the Tuesday. I would now have to go through it all again the next week when I had my Central and RADA auditions.

That Friday morning, I was fast asleep when I was woken by my mother screaming as she ran up the stairs.

"You're in! You're in! Arts Educational have accepted you! You are going to Drama School". It was even better news that I had won a scholarship, and I later found out the Council would pay for my travel and give me an Arts Grant for living expenses. It was all falling into place. I was going to college!

Chapter Two

The first day of the rest of my life

A few years ago, I had the occasion to walk past Arts Ed in Golden Lane. From the exterior it appeared that nothing had changed, but as I walked through those oh so familiar doors, you could clearly see that the facade was the only thing remaining. I was longing to walk in and hear Jackie Bristo shouting her commands as I passed the library, or see Arlene Phillips rushing down the stairs to her next class in the opposite studio. To pass Miss Finch or Miss Rose in the small office to the right of the stairs and bid good morning to them as I ran downstairs to the window shelf where we all met when we were not in class. So many happy and emotional memories.

My first morning at Arts Ed was a mixture of nerves and excitement. In my mind's eye, I had visualised it a thousand times, and it did not disappoint. In my dreams I had been looking down on everything, seeing people rush about preparing for the new term. In reality, I was now in the middle of this over-enthusiastic group of people greeting each other after their summer break, peppered with strangers looking for a place to stand so they wouldn't get run over by the herd of theatrical teenagers.

From day one it was a thrilling experience which I shall never forget. We were all instructed to go to the auditorium of the theatre and wait for the beginning of term introduction.

The first person I remember, was a very confident girl called Rachel Izen. She seemed to be calm and was definitely what my mum would call a no nonsense person. After a while, our heads of departments were introduced to us. They welcomed the new second year students and told them to wait in their seats while Bernard Jameson our Head of Year, read out the names of the new first years, including Rachel's and mine. We went upstairs to one of the small studios on the second floor and were given timetable forms to fill out. As Mr Jameson was explaining how to get to class, Rachel stood up.

"I'm sorry, I think there has been a mistake, I don't think this is the correct course for me. I'm going to swap to the dance class." With that, she picked up her bag and left, leaving a room of open-mouthed students amazed at her confidence.

Mr Jameson continued. "Well let's get started. Go to class."

It was very evident to me after the first day that I had come from being a big fish in a little pond to being bottom of the class. Sidi had done an amazing job with me, and I could pick up choreography and perform a number, but I was now working with people who had either been at stage school for years, or who had been working as child performers, or both. I could dance, but I had no technique. This was going to be one hell of a hill to climb, and I found myself falling behind from day one.

I decided my policy would be to volunteer for everything. It didn't matter how many times I fell down, I would fall, get up and question myself. "What did I learn from that? How can I get better?" Luckily, the college and Bernard Jameson were also behind me. I was given private ballet classes every day with extra singing lessons. I was going to catch up if it killed me.

A chance meeting

Weeks turned into months, and I gradually got used to the muscle pain that greeted me every day. On the morning after my first Ivor Maggido class, I could hardly walk. Now I was only a bit stiff and just needed to stretch out to ease the pain. There was not much time for a social life as we started classes at nine thirty in the morning and finished at six in the evening but, on the odd times Martyn and I did escape, it was often to The Imperial, our favourite little pub in Richmond, Surrey. On one occasion, we were both stood in our usual spot near the side door and next to the jukebox, when a man stopped by on his way out.

"Excuse me. I don't suppose you're an actor are you?" His name was Michael Richmond and he was going to be the director of the Orange Tree Fringe Theatre's summer musical, *Shoot up at Elbow Creek*. He asked me to pop in for an audition the following week. That show was to be my first ever professional job. Luckily, it was in my summer break, so Arts Ed allowed me to do it.

Thinking back, I believe doing that show rather ruined my second year as I had a taste of working and wanted more. Fortunately, I didn't have to wait that long.

In that second year, I did rather feel as if the college was just re-teaching the same things we had learnt in the first year, apart from more performing and, therefore, a lot more rehearsing. By now I was receiving an hour's private singing lesson every day, thanks to Mrs Jack, so my days had become a lot longer. Even so, I was still loving it.

One evening, a group of us decided to take a trip to see the new musical, *A Chorus Line*. We sat in the Upper Circle transfixed. I was watching what my life was to become, and I longed for that life to begin.

Falling downstairs with a honeypot on my head

One of the best things about my second year at Arts Ed, was that we were allowed and even encouraged to audition for shows.

"It will be good for you. Treat it as another class, but don't take anything until you talk to me first." Miss Fisher had said to me. Being tall, slim and able to sing, I got a job within weeks with a dance group touring Italy.

Miss Fisher wisely told me not to take it. "There will be lots of jobs like that. Hold out for something better that will forward your future plans."

Just before our Christmas break, I went to Covent Garden, along with about five hundred other dancers, to audition for a convention for Walt Disney UK; they wanted twelve dancers. We all danced and smiled. You have to smile a lot if you want to work for Disney. After several hours of dancing and, yes you guessed it, smiling, I was chosen to be one of the first ever European *Kids of the Kingdom*. It was a very happy contract and led to me working for Disney and even doing my first ever professional choreography job with them.

When I was working on and off for Disney, I used to do occasional character or skin work outside the Disney cinema that used to be in St Martin's Lane. I could often be seen dressed as Pluto, Goofy, or Baloo the Bear. It was a love hate thing playing Pluto. If you played him on a Saturday you got extra money because you did the 'Mickey Mouse Birthday Club'. The bad news was, when playing him on a Birthday Club day, you had to enter from the back of the auditorium on your hands and knees, whereupon you would be hit, sorry, 'patted' by hundreds of kids as you made your way to the stage.

Occasionally, I played Winnie the Pooh. The logistics of getting in and out of the Winnie costume on your own, were impossible. First you had your legs and feet; the legs were baggy trousers on braces, the feet you slipped over the stirrups at the bottom of your pants. The head and body rested on your shoulders; the only way to see out, was to look out of the word 'Honey' on the pot that was placed over your head. Normally, you would shake numerous hands when dressed up but, as Pooh, the hands were so low down that I had two old wooden coat hangers as arms and hands to wave about. It was like walking about in a barrel. Health and Safety? I don't think so!

On one occasion, I was standing at the top of the stairs dressed as Winnie with a honeypot on my head, waving at the children with their mums and dads, when a coach load of over-excited Girl Guides came hurtling towards me, pushing me down a flight of about fifteen stairs. I don't know who was more surprised, me or the Girl Guides, at the profanities coming from the honeypot!

Chapter Three

Down but never, ever out

Have you ever had a 'sliding doors' moment? A moment of afterthought that is filled with "If only I had done this. If only I had gone earlier"? I had those thoughts for many years, but I didn't do any of the things I dreamt of, in the land of hindsight. Not on that night in Margate. This part of my story will not be peppered with 'if only'. It happened. End of.

Not what you would call the Big Time, but I was off to do a Summer Season in Cliftonville, Margate, working for the notorious cheapskate, Bunny Barron. He and his wife Lisa used to come to our college every Christmas and summer to choose dancers for panto and summer seasons. I was lucky enough to be around when summer shows were still big, every seaside resort had a least one show on. The big show in Margate that year was *The Freddie Starr Show*. I was down the road in the small end-of-pier type theatre, The Lido Theatre, Cliftonville. It was a dump. No doors on the dressing rooms and if it rained it flooded, but I had my provisional Equity Card, that elusive card. It's bizarre when you think how the system worked back then. To get a card, you needed a contract. To get a contract, you needed a card. When you had your first card, you had to work forty weeks until you got your full card. With a full card you could work in the West End. I do agree with the concept of it all, it meant that the theatres were full of people who were actually in the business, they didn't just give them away on the last day of training. Having the card meant something to me. I was on my way.

To be honest, it wasn't great from the first day. The show was called *Take a trip with Jack Tripp*. Our star hated me on sight. It may have something to do with the fact that his partner Alan, who was in the show, took a shine to me. Not in a 'fancy me' way, but he was kind and often came over to talk to me during breaks. Jack would glare at me every time Alan came my way and, when numbers were being set, I was always chosen to be at the back. I was not happy but, hey I was working and would have seven weeks on my card.

The show opened. The rest of the cast on the whole were very nice to me, and I kept my head down and out of Mr Tripp's way. In those days, all the summer shows would socialise together and I became friendly with Barry Hopkins, a singer in *The Freddie Starr Show*. Barry introduced me to Freddy, who liked me. I used to go and blow dry his hair a few times a week, and I was always invited when Freddie was having a meal out or a party. Things were looking up.

Freddie started hiring films, to be shown in the Queen's Hall just below the Winter Gardens Theatre. The first week it was *Young Frankenstein*. I loved it. It was great being in a crowd again, it reminded me of my college days and that feeling of being part of a family group. The following week he hired another film, and we were all meeting before going out for a meal. Normally I would have gone straight from our theatre to Queen's Hall, but that night I had a new white and red top I wanted to wear, so I went back to my digs to change. It was a hot evening and I wore the new top with my tight white jeans. I walked along the seafront without a care in the world.

"Fucking poof" was the first thing I heard. "You queer fucker." I kept walking. I was only a few feet away from a bar we used

17

to go to, I decided would go in and wait it out. The glass hit the back of my head and I fell down, the next thing I was aware of was a kick in my face and side. The rest became an underwater kind of moment and I felt no pain as one of the guys stood on my head. My body had just shut down. When it had all finished, I got up and looked around, I had attracted quite a crowd.

"Please help me." I remember saying and, to my disbelief, everyone just walked away. They didn't want to know. I think that hurt me more than the kicks.

I got to Queen's Hall and Andrew, the other boy dancer, took me to hospital. The cast all rallied around me and were so nice. Mr Tripp asked for me to be sacked, but Bunny Barron refused.

For years I told everyone that I was mugged. Why? Because I was ashamed that I had been 'queer bashed'. I'm not ashamed anymore, and I have claimed the experience back. It was a lesson in life, maybe not the best way to be learning about our world, but I think in a way it made me stronger and never the victim.

I was moving on. The next week, I had a phone call at my digs. I was going to be the production singer in the biggest nightclub in Rome.

You have to travel the world to find your way home

I was always the sort of person who would push themselves. Not so much today, but back then I had a fire in me. I was determined that my life was never going to be full of missed

18

moments; even as a teenager I was always aware of people telling me to live life, as time goes by so quickly. When a contract came along for me to work in Rome, I grabbed the opportunity with both hands and was determined to enjoy and learn from this adventure.

I arrived in Italy with no knowledge of the language or its culture, but as my dad would always say, "If you've got a tongue in your head, you'll never get lost." Well, thank God for the English businessman in the seat next to me on the plane, or I would never have found the small pension I was staying in, let alone the nightclub where I was going to be working.

On my first day at rehearsals, I didn't really have much time to think, we started straight in, learning dance routines and lines of the songs I was to perform. All the girls seemed to be a lot older than me. They weren't, they had just had a lot more experience. I had to learn fast.

Even though my ambition had always been to work in musical theatre, I did secretly harbour a dream to work with showgirls. The idea of walking a Bluebell Girl down a staircase at the Lido in Paris had always been a fantasy of mine, so now The Pipers Music Hall, Rome was going to be my Lido, plus it would help with the weeks of experience which I needed for my Equity Card.

Within weeks, the show was open and I had moved into my little apartment. I had never lived on my own before but took to it like a duck to water, this was going to be fine.

"If you can help anyone get a job in this business, do it" has always been my mantra since I started in my career. I'm pleased to say over the years I have been in a position to help a lot of people further their dreams. I'm a great believer in Karma. "If you do good, you get good."

One night, after our second show, we had a visitor, a choreographer who knew one of the girls. He was looking for a boy dancer. I knew Martyn didn't want to go to college, but that he still dreamt of being a professional dancer.

I thought "Why not? It can't hurt." I put Martyn's name forward. "He can always say no." Within weeks, Martyn had given in his notice from the insurance company where he was working, and became a professional dancer. This was just the beginning of a very successful career.

The next six months just flew by in Rome and it was time to move on, counting the weeks on my card as I went. Next stop, Barcelona!

Barcelona, the time of my life

Rome had been a great experience, but Barcelona was something else. What an amazing city! As a child, I had always predicted that I would live in Spain and here I was, living the dream.

The club we worked in, to say it was sleazy would be an understatement. It was a strip club and we had been brought in to clean the place up a bit. I thought it one big adventure, but I do recall phoning my mum.

"We have four new strippers in the show and three of them are sex changes."

Mum nearly passed out. "Come home. I'll send the air fare." The show was a bit of a mish-mash and I must admit it was rather farcical to be following a stripper, with a selection of songs from *Mame*.

During our stay in Barcelona, I started to have thoughts about going back to the UK and trying my hand at musicals but, all of a sudden, a spanner was thrown in the works. I was offered a contract to work on the cruise liners sailing from New York. I couldn't miss out on this experience, musicals would have to wait a year. Besides, think of the weeks on my card!

That TV show Love Boat has a lot to answer for

I found this entry in an old diary the other month.

"I'm stuck on this bath tub with a load of old people. Everyone is over forty, I'm bored to death!"

How young I was. Only twenty-one and bored. Thankfully, that's something I never suffer from these days. Now it's 'too much to do, not enough time', but when you are young, you want to be out and about with other young people, going to bars and clubs. It's not until you're older and realise that it is all worthless, that stability and security take its place.

The SS Oceanic was a beautiful ship, and we were all treated very well. We had no day duties to do, we had passenger cabins, and ate in the main restaurant. We also only did five shows per cruise, so a lot of the time we were on holiday and being paid. Sounds like bliss now, but in those days I didn't sunbathe or read long books. I wanted fun and I needed stimulation. It was a case of too much of a good thing. One thing we couldn't do was over-eat, as every cruise we were all taken down to the meat scales, and our weight was called out for all to hear. Can you imagine the pressure we were under? We were not allowed to put on or lose four pounds.

As one of the American comedians said "You come on board as passengers, you go off as cargo."

I had to get back to London and start auditioning for shows, my life as a show boy was coming to an end. By the time I got back to the UK, I had over two hundred weeks on my provisional Equity Card. West End, I'm coming to get you!

Chapter Four

Take me to Pantoland

I was home from far-off travels, returning like a conquering hero with Equity Card in hand and a lot of ambition in my heart. One problem. No one knew I was back. I had been away for two years, shows had opened and closed. Some of these I had seen, some I should have auditioned for, when I was working halfway across the world. Apparently, the West End was doing just fine without me.

First thing I did was to get on a train and head straight down to see Martyn, who was appearing in the *Black and White Minstrel Show* at the Pavilion Theatre in Bournemouth. I stayed for five days and was full of my plans for the future. Martyn was going to do panto in Watford after Bournemouth, now I needed to get some work, so out came that week's copy of *The Stage*. I turned to the familiar few back pages; a section I had scanned on many occasions in my youth. This was no longer make-believe, I was now a jobbing actor.

Martyn told me that Bournemouth Pavilion was looking for dancers for panto. That would be perfect, as I knew a lot of the crew. I had a digs' list, but more than that, the stars of the panto that year were to be Polly James and Liz Estensen from the TV series *The Liver Birds*. I loved that programme and was totally star struck. *The Babes in the Wood*, I had to do that production.

If you are going to do a pantomime, you may as well do a big one, and this definitely was a big one. As a child, every Christmas I was transported to the land of fantasy and glamour that we call pantomime when my mother used to take me to see the lavish Palladium pantos or the ice-skating extravaganzas at Wembley. I recall that *Ali Baba and the Forty Thieves on Ice* had been one of my favourites, and I shall never forget the opening of *Cinderella* at the Palladium. The front cloth came alive as the chorus sang 'Welcome to Stoneybroke'. My heart soared. It was bliss. I'm not saying the Pavilion, Bournemouth could be compared to the Palladium, but this was definitely not 'small time'.

Along with the Liver Birds, we had Michael Robbins (Olive's husband from *On the Buses*), Bill Pertwee (*Dad's Army*), the beautiful Sheila Mathews as Robin Hood, a very young Matthew Kelly, Bob Todd (*The Benny Hill Show*) and the person who was to be one of my panto buddies, Su Pollard. I was one of The Jacquie Toye Dancers, four boys and six girls. The John Michael Singers had two girls and four boys or, as we used to call them, ice cream sellers, because all they did was come on stage, stand either side of the proscenium arch in front of a stand mic and sing, looking for all the world like they had a tray of ice creams hidden about their person. On top of all this, we had a full high-flying ballet for six girls. The boys were meant to be in it, but when we saw the brown leotards and balaclavas with beaks, they disappeared very quickly from the number, as did we. Upstaging everyone was the Wonderful Woodland Waterfall. It even had its own dressing room next to ours!

We always knew when it was starting, as all the mirrors shook and cards would fall off the wall. Our dressing room was like heaven to me. Having spent two years working with showgirls, I found myself surrounded by theatrical anecdotes, shocking stories of West End backstage life, and tales of true theatre history. I was eager to absorb all this information and I relished every moment. The main storyteller in our room was Aubrey Budd, his quick wit and razor sharp tongue showed itself on our first day of rehearsals when John Iles, one of the Merry Men, was trying to execute a very basic dance step without much success.

Aubrey turned to me and whispered "She'll be fine when she takes the callipers off."

You may have heard people describe the cast they work with as their family. It could have something to do with our nomadic lifestyle, travelling from camp to camp, bonding within hours, then travelling on a while later. Our panto family was my life for now, and I truly loved them.

The original production had been done at the Birmingham Rep Theatre the Christmas before, and we were to have Clive Perry as the same director, a funny little man who mumbled to himself constantly and changed his mind every five minutes. We were now on stage going through all the technical aspects and Clive was working with Bob Todd, explaining how he should set up the running gag, a joke that runs the entire script of the panto. It gets the 'Little Darlings' all worked up and makes them scream even more. The gag was very simple, there was a gate down stage right and anytime anyone came through the gate, everyone had to shout out "Shut That Gate". This was all very well until our first dress run, an open dress as we had a large group of children in with special needs. Bob had been out for a liquid lunch when he came on as Nanny. Please note, he never wore any make up and had the same costume with flat boots for the whole show. He was just going into the bit where he set the gag up, when he decided to go off-script.

"Now boys and girls, if you see that gate open will you shout out and tell me? Will you? Good, because if the wind comes through that gate it goes right up Nanny's fanny!" There was a sharp intake of breath from everyone in the wings, apart from Michael Robbins and Matthew Kelly who were pissing themselves. All of a sudden, Clive Perry had moved his tiny little legs like the wind and was up on the stage next to Bob. Clive whispered into his ear.

Bob stepped back and said "Fuck it. Sorry. I didn't know the mic was on." There were tears running down my face by now.

Bob was a lovely man. He found out I couldn't get home for Christmas that year, so he had his driver drop me off and pick me up from Mum and Dad's. I never forgot his kindness.

If you've ever met or worked with Su Pollard, you will know that what you see is what you get. That's how she is. Loving, thoughtful and wired to the fucking moon. She was playing Fairy Sunlight and, in one performance, she was making her big entrance, arms flaying around, when her wings fell off. Quick as a flash, Pollard looks up.

"Bloody hell, I'll have to walk home now." One thing you can't say about her is that she is stupid, she is definitely not that, but she's not great at instructions. One morning, Pollard had a casting for Pebble Mill Studios Birmingham. I stayed with her all night so she would wake up for the train at 5.30am. She went off to the call and I went back to bed. We only had one show that evening, and at the half hour call there was still no sign of Su. She only just arrived on time. Su had been in Birmingham, the casting was in London. That's Pollard!

Going back to Mum

There was a definite shift in the atmosphere in our little dressing room. The season was coming to an end and we all needed to work. Agents were calling and auditions were being planned. All I had was the trusty *Stage* newspaper. It had all happened so quickly on my return from the ships that I had no agent. It was another Catch 22 situation, I needed an agent to get good work, but no agent would take me on until I had a job. It had to be open calls again. One of the boy singers was going up to town for his second call for *Sweeney Todd*, another was trying for an opera company. I had no mortgage as I was living back at home, but I still needed to work. I had to try and get into musicals.

On arriving back home, the phone rang. It was Sidi. "How do you fancy coming to dance the Hornpipe for me in Carousel for Watford Operatic?" When Sidi calls, you say yes. The only problem was the show was on in three weeks and only had four rehearsals. I don't think I have ever been so nervous as that first night, not just because I was winging it in most of the numbers, apart from the solo in the Hornpipe, but because in the audience were Aubrey and Pollard. I knew only one of them would behave and, when I saw what Su was wearing, I guessed it wasn't going to be her. A yellow knitted short dress, a man's black tuxedo, a bowler hat, striped tights, yellow tap shoes and a red plastic squirty tie. God help us, one and all.

The show had finished and Aubrey had beaten a hasty retreat. Su was waiting for me at the bar. Luckily, Su is not a big drinker.

"Remember what I said about swearing?" I said. "You can say bloody and that's it, ok?" Su assured me everything would be fine. At that point, Allan Baldwin, the Chairman of the Operatic Society (a well-known solicitor, very posh) came over to meet Su. Here we go.

"Oh hello Allan, I thought the show was fucking marvellous."

A flustered Allan replied. "Did you like our leading man? He's very handsome isn't he?"

"Fucking gorgeous, is he your type then?" She squirted him straight in the eye with her plastic tie.

Things did get a little calmer later on, although I do remember a very odd conversation between Pollard and my mum about joints. Su thought they were talking about drugs and Mum thought it was about lamb. Not that Su needs drugs of any kind, she is high on life. I still see her from time to time, and thankfully she has never changed.

My trip back to 'am dram land' had been fun, but I needed to get an agent and a job. The job came along quite quickly but the agent had to wait a while. The first person I saw as I walked into the audition was Aubrey, always good to see a familiar face. Jan Lynton, the choreographer, was lovely and I could tell she liked me. At the end of eliminations, I found myself in a line-up of four boys, one of them being Aubrey, and four girls. It looked like I was going to do a long summer season on the Isle of Wight.

A few weeks later I met up with Aubrey on the evening *The Stage* was published. We were in The Shaftesbury, a pub in Saint Martin's Lane, frequented by single gentleman who were close to their mothers, and every out of work actor in town.

"Darling, I've got an audition for "Chicago" at the Cambridge. If I get it, I'll have to drop out of summer season. Why don't you come along and try out with me?" In that second, something happened that I had never encountered before. Doubt. What if I'm not good enough? What if in a few hours of auditioning I find out I'm not West End material? I didn't go. Aubrey did, and was cast. He told me I would have easily got the job.

Chapter Five

Bingo and Comedy Heroes

The Isle of Wight was not what you would call a hub of culture, or a magnet for the cream of the witty society folk to gather, but you could hear the bingo being called from the girls' dressing room every evening, and the chips were the best. By the way, I hate bingo! Here I was on Alcatraz, that's what we called it. You could never escape, as the last ferries left before our show finished. Looking back at the show now, it was just a good old-fashioned summer season and we did great business. The show consisted of us as the dancers, comic Peter Goodwright, and a singing duo called Stella and Bambos. She looked and sounded like Nana Mouskouri. He looked as if he'd been dead for a few weeks and she had just dug him up to do the show, we called them Stella and cart horse. There was also a U.V act called Emerson and Jayne with their flying carpet, they were a lovely old couple who lived in a caravan. The show had different headliners every few weeks.

When you have watched these comedy giants as a child, you hope they will live up to your expectations when you work with them. Most of them did, but one definitely didn't. Our first top of the bill was the multi-talented Billy Dainty, a charming and funny man who threw himself into company life, coming for drinks and meals; a really nice guy. A completely different kettle of fish came along when Ted Rogers joined the cast. He was a very quiet and reserved man, we hardly saw him during the two weeks he was with us. After he left, one of my all-time favourites arrived on the island, Frankie Howerd. He was just as I had hoped, a kind, thoughtful person who on his first night took the entire cast out for a meal.

He sat us all in a big square so we could see each other and then said "Right. You all know about me, now I want to know about this rabble. Scott you go first." It was a great evening and we were all sorry to see Frankie leave, even more so when his replacement turned up.

Many times I had sat in front of our old black and white television in Oakdean Road, Watford, and watched Britain's own Norman Wisdom, and now I was going to work with him. My illusions were shattered within seconds of our first encounter.

"And you can get those fucking dancers out of the wings. I'm not having them there putting me off. Go on. Piss off." I don't think anyone of us spoke to him again, not even a Good Morning or Good Evening. Nothing. He spent his whole day out playing golf if I recall, when he arrived at the theatre he went straight to his dressing room and then left immediately afterwards. The only good thing about having him in the show was that we only opened the second act and then left the building. I did stay back one night to catch his set. I must say it was sheer brilliance, such a shame he was a shit.

The day Mr Wisdom left the island, one of my childhood heroes arrived, Leslie Crowther. He was a nice man and he also had the best stories to tell. He would often regale tales of when he worked in Variety and stayed in digs. One of my favourite stories of his involved a certain landlady who had many house rules, one of them being not putting the chamber pot back under the bed after night use, as the steam rusted the springs. On another occasion, Leslie was telling us of a holiday in Spain with his wife. Every evening he used to go out for a stroll and pop into the local gay bar, he would spend an hour or so chatting with the very camp barman and have a night cap. On his last night, he took his wife in with him.

"This is my wife." said Leslie to the barman.

The barman snapped around, gave her the quick up and down and said "It's amazing the things you pack on holiday that you don't need."

Leslie could be very naughty, he could often be found in the wings with one of the girl's finale headdresses on, trying to make us laugh. He was an expert in Polari, a language used backstage by chorus boys, believed to have originated in the fairgrounds and on the ships. Aubrey had taught me some in panto. One performance, Leslie used it throughout the whole show. We loved it. The audience hadn't got a clue.

Escape from Alcatraz

Half way through the run, John Redgrave, our beloved leader and producer, asked us if we would go to Plymouth on our day off and do a few numbers for a charity show for the old Palace Theatre. Any excuse to get off the island, so on the Sunday morning we all packed up costumes, shoes and make-up, and took the show on the road. We arrived in Plymouth just in time to do a run through and sound check before we were on. We treated it as bit of fun, not work but an escape from our day-to-day routine, and a change from dear old Sandown. Next morning, we were up and on our way back, when all of a sudden the words 'cream tea' came into the conversation. That was it, we found a good tea room and had a great time stuffing our faces with scones and jam, and endless cups of tea. We were having such fun that time just ran away with us. The show started at 7.30pm, and we had to be on the ferry by five. Not a hope in hell, we arrived back in Ryde at seven in the pouring rain and with only one taxi. The girls went ahead with the costumes while we were left behind praying for another cab. Needs must, we had to start getting ready, so to the great amusement of our fellow travellers, make-up boxes were opened and we all started dipping our sponges in the puddles. We arrived at the theatre at 7.25pm, put on our wet costumes (the boxes had leaked and everything was soaking) and we made it by the skin of our teeth. The management were told it was heavy traffic; we all knew it had been heavy cream.

At last my sentence was over, and I was going home. Actually, it had been a very nice season. A long one, but I had spent the summer with a great bunch of people and that time on the island had given me a chance to think and get my act together.

Back to Watford, to start looking for an agent and work. I had to be realistic, I was not going to get a great agent straight away, as I had been working abroad for two years, then on the Isle of Wight away from all the auditions. I needed to be London-based. I had an interview with a small agency called Dancers. I was successful and got in, but that didn't last long as we didn't get on at all. I moved to Trends Management after a bit of discussion, as the owner of Dancers had told them I was difficult. After explaining that it was just a clash of personalities, Trends auditioned me and took me on their books. Actually they were very happy to take me as I had already signed for panto, and was going to give them a small percentage of my fee as a sign of goodwill. The great news about panto was that it was in Richmond, so a London gig. I would be free to go to auditions and castings, and I could live at home. Within a few weeks, I had started to audition for musicals.

At last, it was starting to happen for me. I was only 23 and if I just wanted to dance, I only had another few years left to perform. Thankfully, I had inherited my dad's tenor voice. I was on my way and eager to see what the world had to offer.

How many pairs of tights does one dancer need?

From the moment I stepped into the lounge of Terry Parsons' house in Watford for my first costume fitting, I knew that if nothing else, this panto had a lot of money thrown at it. Each outfit I tried on was more elaborate, my finale costume alone was worth a ticket; it was a beautiful gold Henry VIII style tunic with cape, hat and gold boots. Each costume required a different pair of tights and I landed up with seven in varying colours. If the dance routines weren't demanding, the costume changes would be.

As soon as we started work on the show, I realised that the reason we had such a fabulous wardrobe was because that was it, we had been employed to be walking props, something to hang the very exquisite frocks on. David Barclay was the choreographer, and his idea of setting a dance number was to walk to different parts of the stage, stand for eight counts then move again. Thank God for the work out in the dressing room changing clothes, that was definitely going to keep me fit.

It was a very impressive line-up. Terry Scott was playing Dame, he even did his famous 'Bedtime Striptease' number in the show. Terry had not been well before we started rehearsals, having had a bleed on the brain. This left him with very bad mood swings, one day nice as pie, the next a devil. Bernard Bresslaw (from the *Carry On* films) and Christopher Timothy (*All Creatures Great and Small*) were the two robbers, both nice guys. Bernard was very chatty and it was his fault I missed an entrance for the first time. During one performance, Harold from Hammersmith, that was me, had to be called to the stage three times.

In the end, Eric Flynn, playing the sheriff, came into the wings and said " Are you in the Archery contest or not?" Everyone else thought it funny. I was mortified and Mr Flynn never forgave me.

The star of the show, and one of the nicest people I have ever worked with, was Anita Harris. She was lovely. You could never walk past her dressing room door, which was always open, without her asking after your health or what you did last night. I had the lurgy during the run, and when Anita found out she made me do all my changes in her room, with no regard for her own health. Those costume changes - we had so many and they were so fast. Without a dresser to help, we used to wear our finale tights first then layered all the others on top, meaning I had seven pairs on in the opening and my legs got slimmer as the show progressed.

My panto pal for the season was Roy Asbey or, as we called him, Mr Powder Puff, he was always washing his private bits and smothering them with talcum powder. Our favourite number was the end of Act One 'The Hall of Chivalry'. Anita was dressed in a purple cat suit covered in diamante chain-mail with a silver helmet covered in thick purple curled ostrich feathers. We had enormous purple and orange capes with massive hats. Boy, did we work those costumes. Our least favourite number was the animal ballet. I was a fox and Roy, an owl.

Before one performance, we had been told to be more animated, so it came to the part when I had to turn to the back and one of the woodland gauzes reveals a normally passive Mr Owl. "Hoot, fucking, Hoot". He was never given a note again.

It was during this season that Phil Compton, one of the other company members, and I decided to take a trip to Wimbledon to see our old friend Frankie Howerd in panto. The show, as I recall, was a bit tacky but Frankie was the undoubted star. His charm and talent flowed over the footlights making the whole audience believe that he was performing just for them. After the show, we went back for tea and a catch up. We had been sitting chatting for a few minutes when a knock came at the door.

"Oh sorry boys, I forgot to tell you. I have more guests, I hope you don't mind." The door opened and in walked Cilla, her husband Bobby and the boys. I sat there having tea with two of my childhood heroes. I should have felt nervous or out of place, but in fact it was a lovely, relaxed half hour, just a few friends spending time together. When I think back now, the word surreal comes to mind.

Away from the theatre, I was at last being seen for musicals, oddly enough one of the shows for which I had three recalls was *Jesus Christ Superstar*. I say oddly, because I was up for the role of Caiaphas, who sang bass, and at that time I was a high tenor, but hey I'd play anything if it got me into a musical. Both Martyn and my pantos closed, and we decided to rent a flat together. We found a small, two bedroom flat above a junk shop in Harlesden. It was a shithole, but it was ours.

Chapter Six

Time to travel to Scotland to find the king

Since the age of twelve, Martyn and I had talked about sharing a flat, so 121 Acton Lane was our little piece of paradise. As long as you didn't look at the area, decoration, or the damp, it was pretty much perfect in our eyes. On our first full weekend we painted the whole place from top to bottom, even the gas meter got a lick of paint. There can't have been many flats in Harlesden that had a black, pink and gold hallway. It may have looked out of place over a junk shop, but we loved it. It didn't take us long to start auditioning for shows and soon after, we both found ourselves in a musical in Edinburgh.

King of Hearts is a musical set in a small French town in the last days of the First World War, and is based in and around the local mental asylum. We went into town and bought the LP record, and played it every hour God sent. There was a number in the show that called for the can-can, so Martyn and I spent most evenings stretching and practising lifts, heaven knows how we didn't kill each other. Pretty soon it was time for us to fly up to Scotland, which was an adventure in itself and probably the worst flight I had ever taken. Eventually, we arrived at Mrs Macbeth's house in Danube Street and settled in, ready for our first day's rehearsals.

Being part of a musical is like being part of something organic. Watching it grow and develop, taking your ideas and incorporating them with your fellow actors' interpretations. It's far more satisfying than being a dancer, where you just count and conform to be the same as the person next to you. I had enjoyed my time dancing to that drum, but now I was going to do what I had been trained for. One of the most valuable lessons that Hilary Wood, my drama teacher, had taught me, was to observe, sit back and watch the other cast members, not to see what they were doing right, but what they were doing wrong. The room next to the Usher Hall in Edinburgh that morning was overflowing with experience and talent. After heeding Miss Wood's advice, it was apparent that this was a group of benevolent and giving people, who were aiming for a happy and pleasant experience, and boy did we laugh.

Having spent two years doing improvisation at Arts Ed, I was familiar with the technique, but it was all new to Martyn. On our second Monday, Peter Link, one of the writers who was over from the States, decided we should do an improvisation class to determine what character we were from the mental institution. I spent the whole class trying to avoid Martyn's gaze and I was fine, as long as I kept out of his way. At the end of the class, I was cast as a painter. Martyn and Suki Turner, who had spent most of the lesson curled up laughing, were to be acrobatic circus performers. How they got that from two people pissing themselves for an hour and a half, I will never know.

The story of the show is very sweet. It demonstrates how innocence and vulnerability are much nicer qualities than hate and anger. The show has a beautiful number when all the inmates leave the asylum for the first time in years, and go into the real world looking for their king. The number called for us to whistle the first twenty odd bars, the only problem was none of us could whistle.

"What the hell is happening here?" boomed Ed Coleman, our larger-than-life Musical Director. "Can't anyone fucking whistle?"

I had an answer for everything of course. "It's a gay thing."

Ed, who was an absolute treasure, smiled and said "What?"

"Look it's a gay thing, we can't catch balls and we can't whistle. It's genetic." I think it took about ten minutes for the room to calm down. In the end, the orchestra had to whistle from the pit.

One very off the wall bit of casting was to have Martyn and me as two German soldiers. You can imagine the pandemonium when, at the opening of the show, we had to climb out of a trap door with trench coats, helmets and a life-size rifle. It took about five minutes just to get out of the bloody thing. We did try and take our German soldier roles seriously. At one point we had to fire the guns on stage and we had lessons on how to use the weapons. The instructor told us that we mustn't have our mouths closed or it would damage our ears. We were so frightened of the damn things, you could have put a fist in our mouths and you would still have room.

King of Hearts is still on my list of happy shows after all these years.

The show everyone wanted to do.

Every now and then, a musical comes along which everyone wants to be involved in, a piece of theatre that just has that something extra. *Mack and Mabel* was such a show. I nearly wasn't involved in this production, a show that changed the path I took in life and a musical that will always live in a small corner of my heart.

When Martyn and I returned from Scotland, we were about to settle back to normal life again when Martyn had an audition to join the national tour of *Joseph and his Amazing Technicolor Dreamcoat*. He auditioned on the Tuesday and was in the show by the weekend.

There I was in the flat in Harlesden, with no playmate and the usual rounds of auditions starting again. One day, my agent called to say they were casting for the British premier of the Broadway musical, *Mack and Mabel*. I had been a fan of the music for some time, as was anyone who was a fan of musicals. The show had a troubled history and had never had the critical acclaim that its writers, Jerry Herman and Michael Stewart, had wanted but apparently they had rewritten this new production which was destined for the West End.

I sat at the top of the stairs waiting to go in to sing and was surrounded by girls being seen for Mabel, most of them West End veterans. Diane Langton, whom I had seen in *A Chorus Line*, had just belted out a Broadway classic and it was my turn. Wow, this was big time. If I could get this show, I could be London bound. Everything went to plan. I sang and then they asked me to wait and dance with about twenty other guys. I left and started the dreaded waiting game. Nothing happened.

When the phone did ring again, my agent had a casting for me for The British Fashion Awards with Malcolm Goddard staging the show. It was something that I really wanted to do. At the casting, I got talking to one of the girl dancers and she told me *Mack and Mabel* was fully cast. It looked like that was it and the West End would have to wait again. My interview lasted about ten minutes and the next thing I knew, I was booked and being measured for outfits. I left the office floating on air, modelling was another thing on my wish list and I was going to start right at the top. As I entered our little flat, the light was flashing on the answer machine.

It was my agent. "The Nottingham Playhouse has been on the phone, they have been looking for you for weeks as they lost all your details. They are offering you *Mack and Mabel.*" Long before mobile phones, laptops and Google, my fate had been written on a piece of paper thrown away by mistake. I later found I had been cast on the first day and they were about to re-cast when they found me.

The Guildhall in the Barbican was the venue for our meet and greet, there were a few friendly faces including Bronwyn Stanway and Suki Turner from *King of Hearts*, Jonathan Kiley with whom I had worked the Disney contract, Lisa Jacobs from Arts Ed, and Carol Ball who I knew from when Martyn had done panto with her. The charming and charismatic Denis Quilley came over to introduce himself, and the tiny bundle of energy who was to be our Mabel, was an unknown actress by the name of Imelda Staunton. You could just smell success in the air. The director was Richard Digby Day, and choreography was in the very capable hands of Gillian Gregory.

Rehearsals went like a dream. We laughed and cried and laughed some more. On our second week, we had a big surprise as Jerry Herman and Michael Stewart arrived from the States to sit in on rehearsals, both charming and very approachable guys. On a few occasions, I had to pinch myself to believe that I was sitting next to the man who had written *Hello Dolly* and *Mame*, and that we were chatting about shopping and the British royal family. On one occasion we were having supper in the local gay club, when Gary Lyons started talking about the Broadway smash hit *42nd Street*.

He turned to Michael and said "I hear it's amazing, have you seen it?"

Michael smiled at Jerry. "I wrote it Gary."

Things were going well with us, the cast, but tensions were running high with the writers and the production team. Many of the changes and cuts from the original script were either going back in again or just being ignored. Some of Hugh Durrant's costume designs were to be changed and scenery was cut, it seemed a constant battle. The big problem was the ending. In the original ending, as in real life, Mabel dies. Jerry wanted it changed to have a happy ending, so a compromise was reached. On the first preview Richard went out front and told the audience they would see two endings that night, the original sad one and the new, more uplifting one when she lives. The audience would then get a chance to vote for the ending they preferred. They voted for the original ending.

Jerry and Michael were not happy, and we didn't see much of them after that.

The local reviews came out and we were a smash. We were called into the auditorium before the show and told that a producer was interested in taking the show in to the Queens Theatre. None of us were to take any other contracts, they were just waiting on the national reviews. Jack Tinker from the Daily Mail was on holiday, so they sent a deputy who hated it. As I recall, the review went something like this.

"*Mack and Mabel* is a love story without passion, a musical without one memorable song and if the Keystone Cops were alive today, they would arrest the whole company for impersonating comedians."

The transfer to the West End was off, the show closed, and we all moved on.

Chapter Seven

Lady Luck smiling on me again

The show finished on the Saturday and Bronwyn Stanway gave me a lift back to my little flat in Harlesden. I had the after show blues badly this time, they hit me on the Sunday evening. When you have enjoyed doing something so much with so many great people, it leaves you with a terrible empty feeling. Martyn was still out on tour, so I had the place to myself. Monday morning came, and I took myself to the local dole office to organise my next signing-on day and settled in for another period of what actors call resting time. I would have loved to stay in Nottingham for their next musical production *Lady in The Dark,* but it was not to be, as the director wanted to use his own people.

The following day, I happened to be walking in Victoria. I often walked around town, a habit I've never really lost to this day. I passed the stately building that is the Victoria Palace Theatre, a structure I have always thought strangely out of place with its fellow buildings, as if it was just dropped there by mistake, even more so today. Outside the stage door was a House Full sign covered with a large piece of white paper stuck on badly with tape. The sign read 'Auditions this way'. As I have always been of a curious nature, I popped my head around the stage door.

"Excuse me, what are the auditions for?" As I asked this, a rather flustered young man came through the pass door.

"Are you next?" I was told they were casting the first national tour of *Annie.* Auditions were running ahead of schedule and there was a place free now. There I was, with no music and no audition clothes, but I was never one to let an opportunity to pass me by.

I walked on to the now familiar dark stage of an empty theatre, albeit a theatre with which I was not very intimate, being one of the very few theatres in London where I had not even seen a show. Most backstage areas look the same and even smell the same. I can assure you that the glitter and glamour of showbiz does not exist in the wings, and not in the dressing rooms of any 'palace of entertainment' that I have ever worked in.

"What's your name and what are you going to sing?" They were going to remember me when I told them my story. After we went through the whole no music business, they told me the pianist would probably know something I could sing. I approached Lesley, a well-known accompanist at auditions, asked her if she knew anything from *Mack and Mabel*, and we settled on 'Look what happened to Mabel'. I stood stage centre and started.

"Stand still!" came a man's voice bellowing from the middle of the stalls.

"Sorry what did you say?" I was told to stand still, put my hands in my pockets and sing. He later explained that he wanted to hear me sing and my performance was distracting. Strangely enough, I understood what he was talking about and from that day on, I would always stand and sing, not like a robot but, with ease and with a small amount of manufactured confidence to let them hear my voice. I have given this advice to many of my students over the years. It takes a brave and confident performer to just stand and sing.

To my great surprise, I was asked to come back after lunch and do a movement audition. I walked the streets of London again until I needed to be back. I was early, of course. I returned to the stage, we did a short dance number and then I was sent home along with everyone else. When I got back to Harlesden, I called my agent to tell her I had been to a casting.

"I know." she said. How the hell did she know? I had only left Victoria about two hours ago. "They have offered you swing and a year's contract."

For anyone who doesn't know what a swing is, it's a role covering for anyone in the ensemble. In the case of *Annie*, it would mean I would have to learn practically the whole show, as all the male chorus members played numerous parts. In America it is regarded as a great honour to be a swing. I was unsure as it's a massive responsibility and a lot of hard work. I had to think about this and I thought about it for a long time.

I signed the contract on the Thursday. This was going to be interesting.

You wait for a bus, then three come along

The week after I had signed my contract for *Annie*, I was offered a week working with The Singers Company doing the *Barber of Seville* and *La Bohème* at the Festival Theatre in Chichester. Unfortunately, it was the first week of rehearsals of the tour. Luckily, the *Annie* management very kindly said I could do the shows and miss the first week. I can't say it was the happiest job I had ever done. The cast consisted of opera singers and, because I was not a trained classical singer, I was treated very much like a third-class cast member, a bit like commercial television dancers were looked down on by the musical theatre performers. It made me feel bad thinking about the way we used to tease the TV dancers and now I was on the receiving end.

"You sing in musicals? Why don't you go train to be a proper singer?" I did have the last laugh when, on one of the final days of the run, we were out having a meal and the conversation was peppered with "When I sang at The Garden and in Milan it has fabulous acoustic."

I happened to ask "So what are you doing next then?" Silence. Apparently, they were all either going back on the dole or busking. "I have a year's contract in a major national tour. Not bad for not being proper singer hey?" I left the table a little taller that night.

The first day of rehearsals started at the Victoria Palace. Theatre folk become a family very quickly, and I was the runt of the litter having missed the bonding that the rest of the cast had achieved in the first week. I felt very much the outsider and sat on my own in the stalls with a script and a very large notepad in my hands. How the hell did I do this? Should I learn one person at a time or each scene as it is set? They didn't bloody teach me this at college. As I was scribbling down copious amounts of notes on my script and pad, I was aware of a man walking towards me, Gerry Tebbutt had been the swing in the original London production and was now rehearsal dance captain for the tour.

"So, you're the swing are you?" I nodded yes. "I hope you're good." He walked off and never spoke to me again during the whole rehearsal period. I worked with Gerry many years later, and we both laughed when I told him the story. He is a lovely man.

It came to lunchtime and I needed the toilet, so I used the stalls' wash room. When I came out, everyone had gone to lunch leaving me in the auditorium, lit only by the working lights spilling over the orchestra pit. I didn't blame them, they just weren't used to having the runt around.

I did know a few people in the cast. Carrie Ellis had been at Arts Ed with me in the year below, and I had known Peter St James for a few years. Other than that, I knew no one, but things changed when costume fittings started. I was expected to stand in for anyone who was not there even the girls, as I found out I was to cover them as well. No, not in drag, but if any of the female cast were off, there would be an extra male servant etc. After a few days of standing in for everyone, I got to know them all very quickly.

One person in the cast was the actor, David Alder, known to everyone in theatre land as Daisy. I had heard many a story about the famous Daisy when I had worked with his flat mate

Aubrey Budd back in my Bournemouth panto days. My favourite theatrical tale about Daisy is a story I reminded him of last year. He tells me he doesn't remember it, but says it's probably true. I do hope so as it's a lovely story. Aubrey and David were auditioning for a panto many years ago at the end of the final line up.

The choreographer had everyone in a semicircle and asked "OK I can see you can all dance, but does anyone do any acrobatic tricks, back flips or cartwheels?"

At this point, Aubrey stepped forward and said "Daisy can".

"Daisy fucking can't!" replied a flustered Mr Alder.

Getting myself into the swing of it all

I was beating myself up about being swing on the show, until in the end I became so anxious I had stopped eating and wasn't sleeping at all. The not sleeping bit I could cope with, but I certainly didn't want the old demons of my eating disorder to reappear. At college we were all constantly being told we were too fat, and as a result I stopped eating. No breakfast, then an apple and a piece of cheese for lunch. My evening meal consisted of a saveloy that I would pick up at our local chippy in Sudbury Town. I lived on that whilst I was still doing class for around seven hours a day. I liked the feeling of being hungry, it gave me some power over my life and in any situation I found myself.

When people said things like "You are so thin, I'd love to have your figure." it made me feel good. I needed to take control of being the swing in the show, so those old feelings wouldn't start to enter my mind again. Luckily, things changed by one tiny statement, a few words from Peter Walker, our director.

We were in Bristol on the first date of the tour and opening night had arrived. Backstage was the usual chaos of cast and crew running around all on their own little missions to make opening night perfect for themselves, but what was I meant to do? I had no purpose, just the spare to fill the space if someone was ill or on holiday. A voice came over the speaker in the dressing room I shared with Peter St James and Robert Locke.

"Scott St Martyn, could you please go to Ursula Smith's dressing room" I knocked on the door.

"Come in. Oh Scott, I'm so behind getting ready and I know you've got nothing to do, so could you hand out my cast first night cards?" The low point got even lower when I noticed that there was no card for me. As I was handing out the cards I passed Peter Walker and he instinctively knew something was wrong.

"Got five minutes? Let's go and have a drink." We sat in the bar and Peter said "I know it's difficult for you, you may not think it but you are a part of this production." I knew he was trying to make me feel better, but it wasn't really working.

"Peter, why did you choose me to be swing?"

At this point it was Peter's turn to say "Scott, you are multi-talented and should be a big star." but what he actually said was "You are reliable, and you have a reputation in this business for being a hard worker and consistent. That's the best recommendation anyone can ask for. You will never be out of work."

My whole attitude to being swing changed at that moment. Not only was I going to be a good swing, I was going to be the best swing ever. I took my position very seriously and would strive to make all of my performances perfect. Unfortunately, that was not always possible when gremlins got in the way or, occasionally, other actors. Which story shall I start with? So many to choose from.

The way to survive a national tour

If you are embarking on a national tour, do yourself a favour and take David (Daisy) Alder out for lunch and ask him to explain the dos and don'ts of life on the road. I was lucky enough to have Daisy take me under his wing from the very start of my *Annie* experience. Daisy knew exactly how I felt about being a swing, as he had done the same job in town. He would often sit me down and give me tips on every aspect of being an ensemble cover, and how to do the show if more than one person was off at any time. I was dreading this prospect, but Daisy assured me it would happen one day. One of his other tips was how to deal with the ultra-butch 'keep your backs to the walls boys' stage hands who used to dread a musical coming to their theatre in case the chorus boys all held him down and deflowered him. The game was called the Prize Game and it went like this.

Daisy would pick out the gang leader and when he passed would say "Hello Prize" and the next time "Hi Prize".

This would go on until the crew member would eventually say "Why do you keep calling me Prize?"

Daisy's reply: "We were having a raffle!"

By now I had settled into the tour. Not only was I swing, I was now also second cover to Rooster played by Trevor Jones, which meant lots of understudy calls. I didn't mind as it was an opportunity for me to learn the show playing every part, and this was very fortunate because the scenario that Daisy had warned me about, was just about to happen.

Charles West, our Daddy Warbucks was off and Morgan Deare was moved up to play his part. John Lee Green and Tony Rickell were off sick, so I was on for all three of them. Remembering all the actors in the show played multiple parts, and looking at the script, I thought this would be possible if I under-dressed.

I called my parents. "You have got to come up to Birmingham tonight, I'm never going to be on so much. The only one on stage more than me is Annie!"

At the start of the show, I was in the wings looking like the Michelin Man. I had three costumes on, and Go..! On for Bundles, change. On as Assistant Dog Catcher, change. On as Lieutenant Ward, change. On in Hooverville (off half-way through the scene so I could come back on and arrest myself). On as Lieutenant Ward, change. On as Servant, change. On as Father Christmas, change. On as Man in Window, change. On as Lieutenant Ward, change. On as Servant...end of Act One! You get the picture? I can assure you by the end of that performance, I could definitely say that I knew the show.

It didn't run so smoothly on another show when I was covering for more than one actor. On this occasion, I needed help from one of my fellow cast members. We came to the big number in the second act, when the Warbucks' mansion is transformed into a beautiful Christmas scene for Annie to be seen for the first time with the famous curly haired wig and red dress. At a certain point in the number, a ten-foot Christmas tree crosses the stage and then lights up to the applause of the servants on stage. That's what should have happened. The two actors who were meant to push and pull the tree into place, on very specific stage marks, were for this performance to be played by Robert Locke and me.

"All you need to do is push. It's not that heavy, but you will need to give it a good shove at first. I will be on the other end, pulling and putting it on its marks."

Easier said than done. Music cue comes up. Go! Robert pushed with all his might for his small frame and the tree shot across from stage right to stage left in what must have been an Olympic medal time, if there ever were to be such an event. I landed up wedged against the wall by the tree, scattering stage crew as I went, so when the company did turn around, it appeared that Christmas had been cancelled.

The worst thing to happen to any actor on stage is to get a fit of the giggles or corpsing as it is known. My worst ever encounter with this was at the Pavilion Theatre in Bournemouth.

What's in a name?

Let me set the scene for you. We were in Act Two, Annie has just been told that Daddy Warbucks wants to adopt her when, all of a sudden, two people arrive claiming to be Annie's real parents, Ralph and Shirley Mudge. They were really Rooster and his girlfriend Lily in disguise, and they were going to try to extort some money from Warbucks. It was a normal performance on a warm evening in Bournemouth, and I was on again, as I had been frequently that summer. Most of the cast was on stage and I was standing behind the sofa just off centre stage, when Petra Siniawski and Trevor Jones entered as the Mudges. The script continued as usual, until Petra had to tell Annie that she is their child.

"You never knew it dear, but your name is Shirley Mudge." Freeze Frame. What did she say? The whole cast focused on Petra, as it is kind of important that the child's name is Annie! Petra realised her mistake and proceeded to try and dig herself out of an ever deepening hole. Trevor Jones was a mess, he was crying so much that the river of tears was in danger of wiping the fake moustache off his face. I thought he was going to be sick, he was holding his laughter in so much. I was aware that I must not look across the stage at Peter St James or I would also be lost. Too late, I looked over he was shaking so much that the powder he had in his hair to make him look older had formed a cloud above his head. I remember looking down at my hands gripping the back of the sofa and thinking my knuckles were very white as the tears dripped on the back of my hands. I must say the only true professional on stage that evening was the little girl playing Annie, the rest of us were a disgrace.

One of the other performers who was not so professional was Sandy, the dog. The poor thing was fine when we started in Bristol, but by the time we had reached Norwich, it was bored. To break the monotony, he first decided he would ignore the child in the famous number, you know the one. It may have been my fault as I was on as Lieutenant Ward and I had treats in my pocket, so believe me, if you know dogs and there is a choice between a child shouting out a song or a man with food, the dog will choose food. On the whole, the dogs, I say dogs because there were two of them (how showbiz that even the dog had an understudy), were well-behaved, although when they did let Randy the cover on, it was sick on stage and the vomit remained centre stage for the whole of Act One. We were lucky to have any dogs at all after Peter St James and I were asked to look after them when Jamie the dog handler had to go up to town one Sunday. We foolishly decided to take them for a walk along Alum Chine. This was not a good idea as we lost them within five minutes. Luckily, they came back after a few hours. I had played most of the parts by now but wasn't keen on putting on a dog suit.

I always regard the tour as one of my best jobs, and I certainly learnt a lot during my time on the road, but when it was time to start talking new contracts, fate stepped in again.

Richard Digby Day, the director I had worked with in *Mack and Mabel*, came to see the show in Leeds. "How would you like to come back to the Playhouse in Nottingham for the Christmas production of *H.M.S. Pinafore*?" As luck would have it, the tour was finishing in Nottingham at the Royal. I could be on call for *Annie* and do rehearsals at the playhouse in the daytime. This was going to be fun.

Chapter Eight

Never work with children, animals or Nicola Blackman

What this chapter should be called is "Everyone **should** work with Nicola Blackman." Of all the people I have ever worked with in my career, she has bought me more joy, laughter and trouble than anyone else. Surprising, as our initial meeting didn't go what you would call well.

Returning to Nottingham Playhouse felt like going home for me. The whole venue contained so many happy memories, it felt as if I had only been away for a few weeks and not the year it had actually been. On arriving at the meet and greet in the upstairs bar, I was welcomed with a mixture of new and familiar faces. Before the days of Facebook, when arriving on a first day you never really knew who you would be working with, so that day held extra excitement. The air was full of enthusiasm and a lot of hugs and air kissing. As I was chatting with my old friend Bronwyn from my *King of Hearts* and *Mack and Mabel* days, I was aware of a young black girl sitting in the corner, her Walkman earplugs blocking out the barrage of noise echoing round the small anteroom off the bar. She seemed to be unwilling or uninterested in joining in. Later, Nicola told me she found the whole thing, and me, a bit overwhelming as she knew no one. I seemed to know everyone, it was hate at first sight.

As we approached the end of the first week's rehearsals, I found out a little more about Nicola. She was already a 'West End Wendy' having appeared in *Showboat* at the Adelphi Theatre at the age of fifteen. She had just been nominated for

Best Supporting Actress in *Destry Rides Again*. I was very impressed, but not our leading lady, Anna Sharkey.

"I'm going to be late in to rehearsals on Monday morning, I'm going to the SWET Awards (now the Olivier Awards) on Sunday evening." said Nicola.

"Oh, are you doing the catering?" Miss Sharkey replied!

Anna was an odd little thing, totally miscast by about thirty years, but with a lovely voice. A true eccentric, she could be constantly found wandering around the rehearsal space, talking or singing to herself. When we arrived on the stage, her main concern seemed to be her hair piece, her own hair was a dark strawberry blonde but after she enhanced it with a tinting brush it changed colour beyond recognition, leaving the piece four tones lighter. I don't know what Anna saw in the mirror, but it wasn't what everyone else could see.

We were a happy little band and the cast was gelling very nicely. Trevor Jones and I were again working together, we were both leaving the *Annie* tour on the same day and, as before, I was to be his understudy. Also, in the cast, playing the Boson, was a very young Douglas Hodge. The choreographer was the lovely Gillian Gregory, and when she was setting the finale of Act One it looked as if I was in great danger of dancing with 'that loud black girl' as I referred to Nicola. Gillian changed the staging to keep us on opposite sides of the stage. The show opened, and I seemed to have avoided having any real contact with Miss Blackman until one afternoon we just happened to click over a fancy dress costume.

The club, La Chic Part Two, was having a toga party and as I knew everyone would be wearing white I decided to go in black and gold. Now to make my costume, with only one problem that I can't sew. I was standing in front of the mirror draped in black chiffon and yards of gold braiding wondering how the hell I was going to do this.

"Hello heart, can I help?" Nicola stood in the doorway. Why not? I needed all the help I could get. Looking back, I don't know how it happened but in minutes we were laughing and all of a sudden we had become friends, not close immediately, but something had changed.

The show was not without its dramas. Ned Sherrin and Caryl Brahms had been given the task of rewriting the book, adding a prologue about a group of actors on the last vessel of the British navy putting on a production of *HMS Pinafore.* David Steadman had re-scored the show, and a lot of big dance numbers had been added. All was going well until two days before we started dress runs when our leading man, the very handsome David Kernan playing the Captain, up and left the show without warning. To this day, I still don't know why he left. Dudley Stephens was sent for, and took over the part at very short notice; he received rave reviews.

Caryl Brahms died on our opening night. The show closed, and we all went back to our own little homes spread all over the country, saying goodbye and hoping we would all work again together soon. Back to auditions.

Caught short in Leeds

I had only been back from Nottingham a week or so and I was again on the rounds of castings. I'm very grateful that when I was starting out, the repertory theatres were still doing musicals. It's what kept the venues open, that and panto. Luckily they seem to be popular once more in the provinces, otherwise I don't know how the young actors of today would learn their craft. I had learnt so much at college, but being able to work in different theatres with a range of directors, choreographers and other performers was invaluable, and I needed to pay my half of the rent.

The York Theatre Royal had just got the rights to do the first ever repertory production of *Jesus Christ Superstar*. They asked to see me because the director was a friend of Richard Digby Day and he had seen the last night of *HMS Pinafore*. It was one of the easiest auditions I have ever done and the beginning of my long association with *Jesus Christ Superstar.* I was booked to play Annas the priest, and I needed to find digs.

Who did I know who has done lots of work in the provinces? Nicola Blackman! My old college mate, Debbie Goodman, who was Nicola's flatmate at the time, answered the phone and I started to tell her about York, when she covered the hand piece and I could hear her talking to someone.

Next thing I knew, Nicola was on the phone. "Daughter, I'm doing York as well." Believe me, when you know anyone on the same cast list as you and you are looking for digs, a close bond grows very quickly. By the end of the conversation we were going to be sharing and, to seal our friendship, a few weeks later we were both offered *Rocky Horror Show* and *West Side Story*, both back in Nottingham.

This was the beginning of a truly memorable six months. We arrived at rehearsals together and never really left each other's side. I don't think I have ever laughed so much as during those days. It doesn't take much for me to be led astray, but with Miss Blackman I was a willing victim. Every time there was a cry of "Quiet! Keep the noise down." it was invariably aimed at the two of us.

On one of our very rare nights off during rehearsals, we went on a little jolly to Leeds old City Variety Theatre. Martyn was filming the TV series, *The Good Old Days*, and he had managed to get us tickets with invites to the free bar afterwards. I was determined to drink my television licence fee if it killed me. We were to travel in Nicola's old Mini and, being over six feet tall, there was always a comedy moment getting in and out of that thing. It also had the most temperamental heating system. When it was on it stayed on whatever you did, and this was unfortunate for the circumstances that developed later. We had an amazing night and it had been good to get away from work for a few hours. After the show, we went to the bar and waited for Martyn. Danny La Rue was top of the bill that evening and I must say on our first meeting he was charming, but more of my turbulent relationship with Mr La Rue later. The end of the evening came, we said our goodbyes and went to find the car. It was a cold spring evening and as soon as the cold air hit our bladders we both needed to pee.

"Look, there are two industrial dustbins over there, you go behind one and I'll go behind the other."

I followed her instructions, nature was taking place when suddenly a car turned around the corner shining its full headlights on Nicola's bum.

She shot up, screaming with laughter "Oh Daughter, Daughter." The car passed by, with the driver in trauma, I'm sure.

"You ok?"

Nicola was still doubled over with laughter. "Yes, only problem is, I was so busy laughing, I forgot to stop peeing, all over my track suit."

Unfortunately, the car heating was stuck on high the whole journey back to York

Who would have thought a crucifixion could be such fun?

I don't know if it's the same today, but back in the eighties there was a café bar front of house at the beautiful York Theatre Royal and it was very popular with both cast and the public after performances. Nicola and I had hatched a plan to get around any queuing at the end of the show. There is a very moving piece of music called 'John Nineteen Forty-One', which is played as our Lord has just died and the crowd disappears. In our production, everyone apart from the priests, Judas and Jesus left through the auditorium, then ran round to the stage door and came back on for the finale. Fortunately for myself and Nicola, she had to pass the café on the way back to the stage, so in a sombre atmosphere of people crying, the music playing and Jesus on the cross, if you listen very carefully you could hear "Double poached egg on toast with extra toast" as Nicola passed me. My order was ready by the time I'd changed out of my costume.

The protesters outside the theatre would have had a heyday if they had heard the blasphemy throughout most performances. They would have been even more upset by the nickname given to Richard Courtice, the cover for Paul Baden who played Jesus. When Richard had to go on, over the Easter weekend (yes, Paul went sick on Good Friday and was back for Easter Monday!), he had been a cover on the national tour so knew the part well. Everything went smoothly apart from at the Last Supper when he grabbed the hand held radio mic and shoved the lead straight up his noise. It must have hurt. The Friday show was coming to the end and we were up to the crucifixion. Normally when the lights came up, Jesus was to be found on the cross with blood running down his face from the crown of thorns, and a small trickle from the sword wound in his side. Not this night. Richard had gone blood mad and was covered from head to toe in it.

As Nicola passed me that evening, I said "Looks like Jesus has been in a car crash." From that day on he was known as Richard Car-crash.

Time to move on again, it had been a memorable few months in York, but what I will remember most, is that it was the place that cemented a friendship for life.

—

Happy in horror

Little did I think, back in the student days living in Parsons Green when I used to walk to the converted cinema in the Kings Road, that one day I would be involved in a production of *The Rocky Horror Picture Show*. I remember that first venture into the strange world of Transylvanian Transvestites, it certainly wasn't my idea of a musical, having been brought up in the more traditional world of Lerner and Loewe, and high kicking chorus lines. On that one night, my horizons were blown wide open. It felt so different, so like nothing I had ever seen before, even the audience were different, and having always felt at a different angle from all around me, I found myself in an auditorium where I seemed the normal one.

Arriving back home, which was how I regarded Nottingham Playhouse in those days, I was eager to get started. We met in the upstairs foyer on the first morning and were a merry little band from day one. It's much easier to get to know the company when there are only a few of you. One person in particular I clicked with straight away, especially when I found out she was to join Nicola and me in *West Side Story*, the musical to follow *Rocky*, and I'm pleased to say we are still friends after all these years. Rosie Ashe is a West End theatre legend and I'm proud to call her a friend.

"Let's find a house and we can all live together for the summer." Rosie said, in her endearing ever confident manner. By then Martyn had also auditioned for the show and been cast, so the hunt was on for a three bedroom house. Digs' lists were scrutinised and a house was booked for that summer.

Rehearsals were going well and I was getting the hang of working in a wheelchair for my main part of Dr Scott. All was good, until our director Richard Digby Day had the bright idea to have Nicola push me around the stage. Great fun for her, absolute fear for me. I still can't straighten my fingers after they were trapped in the wheels on several occasions.

This was a dream job and I loved playing my two very different parts, Eddie and Dr Scott. Nicola, Rosie and I were now the new very naughty Three Musketeers.

The day of our opening arrived, we had a dress run at 2 o'clock and curtain was up at 7.30. We all thought it went rather well, apart from when I came on as Eddie to sing my number. I was experimenting with blood capsules and I spat blood all over the floor. It worked well and got a good reaction but, unfortunately I spat in exactly the same spot that Rosie had to roll around in when she did her song with Rocky. She was left with blood stains all over the back of her pale pink French knickers, not a good look. I decided to cut the blood capsules down to one not four.

When we finished the dress run, we went down to the auditorium for notes. Richard tore into us, and said he wanted to do another run. By now it was five, leaving us not much time between the dress and opening night. Fortunately, well not that fortunate for Danny Webb the actor playing Riff Raff, he hit his head on a piece of scaffolding on the set cutting himself quite badly. This halted the second dress, giving us the time we all needed to prepare for the first night. The opening was a hit as was the whole run. Danny got back in time from the hospital all stitched up, the bang on his head certainly didn't damage his career as he is constantly on our screens. Every time a new TV series comes on, I look for his name and nine times out of ten he is there.

Time had come for the parental visit. Mum and Dad came to see everything I was in apart from Edinburgh, which was just too far for Dad to drive. It wasn't until the show had started that it suddenly occurred to me that Mum might be shocked by the sexual content in the show. After the matinée, I took a deep breath as I entered the bar.

"So, what did you think?" I was waiting for my mother to rant about the filth she had just witnessed.

"Where did you get those fabulous legs? You didn't get them from my side of the family!" Apparently, my parents were more broad-minded than I thought.

Summer on the West Side

By now Martyn and I had moved from Harlesden to a very smart little studio flat in Baker Street. It was far too expensive for us, but very handy for auditions. When we both got cast in *West Side Story*, we thought it best not to sign a second six month contract but move everything up to Nottingham. We packed everything in Nicola's small car, everything we owned including our budgies, Bona and Palone.

When you get a group of over twenty young performers together in one production, you can guarantee it's going to be messy. I knew this was going to be true when on one of our first Sundays off, word got around that we were having a roast dinner. We started with four of us and ended up with about fifteen. When we ran out of plates, we improvised with trays, even a frying pan was used. Afterwards we played games, at one point during a very animated game of hide-and-seek in the streets, Martyn and I ran into a policeman.

"Have you seen a group of kids playing near here?"

"How old?" was the reply.

"Early twenties" I said.

The original choreographer was to be the Tony award winning Gillian Gregory, but she had to drop out and Stephanie Carter who had just staged *Rocky Horror* took on the job. I was to be her dance captain, a job I had never done before. When you're in this position it can be quite difficult as you're stuck in the middle. I had to keep a certain distance from the dancers, as at some point you will have to tell someone off, as indeed I did. I wanted to share a dressing room with Rosie, but Richard would have no mixed sex rooms, so I shared with a lovely actor who played Doc, Carl Oatley. Poor Stephanie was paranoid that the dancers didn't like her or her work, and she was often in my room in a real state.

West Side had never been on my to-do list. I had not done it as an amateur and had never even seen it professionally but, when we started work on the show, I was hooked. It's a very dark and at times heavy piece, but that didn't stop our little band of trouble from adding a lot of onstage humour to this great masterpiece of musical theatre.

I knew when we started work on the fight scene 'The Rumble', that this could be a danger spot with the gigglers in the cast. The fight director, Sumar Khan, was very strict and ultra-serious, so when one of the boys, Ray Davis, kept calling him Susie, it was only a matter of time before Sumar picked him up by the neck. It wasn't only his new nickname that offended him, it was when he asked us all to vocalise the attack section of the scene.

Sumar overheard Ray screaming at me. "You bitch, you stole my husband." followed by "That's my mascara. You've been in my Dorothy bag again."

Another danger spot was in the 'Somewhere Ballet'. We performed this on a large revolving floor, and were sitting targets for the other cast members, namely Miss Blackman, who at one performance found an adult-size sheep costume in the wardrobe department armed with a water pistol. We went down like floating ducks at the fairground.

It was during the run of the show that Nicola had been cast in the West End production of *Little Shop of Horrors*. Poor thing had to do the show at night and then be up at the crack of dawn to go up to London for rehearsals. This didn't harm her performance in any way at all, there can't be many actresses who have played the minor role of Rosalia and stolen the reviews from Anita, the lead. How did she do it? In the dance at the gym scene, three of us, myself, Sadie Hamilton (playing Anybodys) and Nicola, did not do the dance. Sadie and I stayed at the back doing a lot of angry bored teenager acting while Nicola stayed at the front doing a three act play with her shoe, a bottle of coke and a fan. It was a work of art. I'm sure some of the audience didn't even notice the dance.

The summer had passed and the show came to an end. The good news was that both Martyn and I had been booked to return at Christmas, to be in the cast of *The Gondoliers*.

Chapter Nine

A Christmas Reunion

Christmas of '83 at the Playhouse was like a family reunion for me. The cast of *The Gondoliers* was full of so many familiar faces, Trevor Jones from the *Annie* days, Joan Davis from *Pinafore*, Jane Arden from *King of Hearts*, Amanda Prior from *Mack and Mabel*, Jonathan Kiley from *Disney, Mack and Mabel, Pinafore* and *Rocky Horror*, and Jenny Gregory, Paul Reeves, William Relton, Chris Lang, Rosie Ashe and Martyn, all from *West Side Story*. It was like slipping on an old pair of slippers, comfortable and safe.

The production was beautifully designed once again by Hugh Durrant; the first act being very traditional and the second, modern and set by the swimming pool. Martyn and I had to dance with huge beach balls, while Paul and Chris were on roller skates, all of us wearing swimming costumes. The sold out sign was out most nights and, on the whole, the company were very well behaved, apart from a certain Miss Ashe who made herself laugh so much in the finale at one performance that a small puddle appeared at her feet by the final call. It was one of those casts that liked to party, we seemed to be out every night. It was Christmas every day for us.

The show was sponsored by Mansfield Brewers, and after the show one evening, they had a party for us all. In the centre of the bar was an enormous display of drinks; beers, ciders and soft drinks. At the end of the night, we were told we could take any of the display home for our own consumption. Martyn and I were hosting Christmas at our place that year, we were now living in Shepherd's Bush. We loaded our bags, arms, shoved bottles up our coats and took half the stock back to our digs up the Mansfield Road, near the Goose Fair. When we woke the next morning, we felt so guilty we took it all back, only to be told it was fine and we could keep it. We kept it under our places in the dressing room. It made for a great Christmas.

I knew my time at the Playhouse was coming to an end as Richard Digby Day was leaving to go to America. The end of an era and a new man, Kenneth Allen Taylor, was in charge. Nottingham had been good to me, keeping me employed for a long time with many shows, many friends and many happy memories.

The good old Good Old Days

I loved being on tour. When you are thrown together, you become a family very quickly. The dancers like bear cubs in winter, huddle together and after the second tea break everyone usually finds out that by one degree of separation, they are connected to someone with whom they have worked, or was at their college. I hadn't done a lot of tours, just *Annie* and a fashion show tour. The *Annie* tour was a year long, and we stayed in each place for at least a month. The fashion show was a different town every day, but now I was on a weekly tour of the BBC's *Good Old Days*, and as an added bonus I was touring with Martyn. We had a blast!

The production starred Frankie Vaughan, Jan Hunt, Ted and Hilda Durante, The Duo Lanka and Norman Vaughan. It featured Mr Leonard Sachs as Chairman and us, The Players

Theatre Company. I had only done one episode of the TV show filmed at the lovely City Variety in Leeds. It was the last ever filmed, called *Farewell to the Good Old Days.* Martyn was meant to do it but had other work commitments, so I stepped in. Martyn had done several years of the TV series and had worked at the Players Theatre, under the arches off The Strand.

We stayed in some very old-time theatre digs, memorably the digs in Liverpool where Ted Durante and Jan Hunt told stories at breakfast that went on way past lunchtime. I don't remember the stories, but I do remember we all fell up the stairs, laughing at a very unfortunate family photo on the staircase wall.

Some of the theatres were so vast they had to bring in masking to make our very pretty little set fit the space and not look lost in 2000 seater palaces of entertainment. When performing at the Birmingham Hippodrome, I was talking in the wings during the overture while the rest of the players company were on stage dressed in Ascot costumes for the 'Shayna, At the Races' number. About two minutes into the overture, the house curtain just flew out for no reason and my fellow Players were forced to stand frozen for the remainder of the music, leaving me to practice my best gurning at them from the wings. At the Bath Theatre Royal, the boys in the group were positioned behind a show cloth whilst Jan Hunt was in front giving her Clarince Morgan or as we called her Clarince Ming. The show cloth was meant to fly out on a certain bar of music. It didn't! It flew out about a foot. All you could see was a row of boy dancers jumping up and down calling out to the stage management. "Get it up, get it up." At

---

which point Martyn decided to run round in front of the cloth, stepping over the conduit bar that holds the cloth at the bottom. As he stepped over the bar, the cloth flew out taking Martyn with it, only a few feet, but high enough to make him sing those top notes a little stronger that evening.

Martyn and I should never be allowed to be on a stage together as we are both gigglers. I'm bad, but Martyn is a champion. One week, we were performing on a stage with no rake (a flat stage with no tilt). The Duo Lanka were on before us doing an act that involved balancing golf balls on golf sticks. That night, it went badly wrong and at the end of their spot, there were golf balls all over the stage. This had happened before but, on a raked stage they just rolled to the foot lights and we had no problem with the said balls. Enter Clarince Ming and her boys. It was like a life size ping-pong machine. Martyn and I were a mess. It got so bad that one of the other boys reported us to the company manager in the interval for being unprofessional.

Apart from the time when the radio mics were left on by mistake at the top of the Second Act, and you could hear Jan Hunt telling her dresser how to fiddle the tax man, my favourite memory of that tour was Doncaster. We played in a three screen cinema, albeit that we were on Screen One. Screen two was showing *Christine: Killer Car*, whose sound track was a lot louder than our singing, and the whole show was peppered with car crashes and death screams. Even Frankie lost it. Oh, how we laughed.

Twenty Seven and too old to be in the show!

While still on tour, news hit the streets that a new Broadway show was coming to town. Not just any show, but the blockbuster musical *42nd Street*. I had the LP at home and had played it often. The whole world and his wife would be going for this show, I knew I'd better start practising my time steps. I paid a trip to my agent and asked her to get me an audition.

"You're too old. Sorry, they are only seeing dancers under the age of 22." At the age of 27 I was too old to dance in a West End musical.

"You have not heard the last of this." I told my agent. "Tell them to see me first, then tell me I am too old." I got an audition the following week.

The first audition was held at the Theatre Royal Drury Lane. I have never seen so many dancers in one place. I was later told they saw over 2,000 people at the London auditions alone.

I don't know whether it was something I learnt as an amateur or a lesson we were taught at college, but I always dressed the part for auditions. There I was, surrounded by pink and yellow Lycra, leg warmers and head bands, all very *Fame*, while I was standing proud looking like I had just stepped out of a 1930s movie in Oxford bags, short sleeve shirt, tank top and a bow tie. Even my hair was authentic Brylcreem. I still hate that smell.

We all stood in the, by now familiar, cattle call line up and were told to step forward and do a set of shuffles to the left and right. When everyone had finished, names were called out, but mine was not one of them. Everyone was being dismissed with some being told about details for the forthcoming recalls. I had not come here to be eliminated at the first call.

I walked straight over to one of the two Americans who had been taking the auditions, a tall slim woman with dark hair and glasses. Her name was Karen Baker, she had been one of Gower Champion's assistants on Broadway. She was as tough as nails and she terrified me.

I don't think I would have the guts to do it now, but I was so fired up and so determined to get the job, or at least have a good go at getting it.

"Are you not going to hear us sing?" When I think about it now, it makes me smile at my nerve.

"Excuse me? No, you have not been chosen. You can go now." I was not going to give up. I remained and did not leave until I had told her that I was a strong singer and a tenor, that I had heard the show and knew they would need good singers. How bold was I?

In the end she took my name and said she had made notes about me. I would love to know what those notes said.

Is no one going to answer the phone?

"I don't know what you said at that audition, but they have put you on the stand-by list." My agent was very impressed. She told me they were having the final recalls in a few weeks and, if they couldn't cast all the guys, I would be called back at a later date.

"Let's hope they have cast me."

The following week the phone rang. "They want to see you again, you must have made quite an impression."

I was pleased to find out that my next audition was to be held at the Victoria Palace, a place I was very familiar with as I had rehearsed the tour of *Annie* there. Every little thing helps when you are under the pressure of an audition.

The stage was full of about 25 guys, the same guys I had met at many a call-back. As in the last call, I was dressed to the nines, Thirties mode and, as before, everyone else was in their best Pineapple dancewear.

The choreography for the show is not difficult, there is just a lot of it. The opening number consists of a lot of different time steps done in an American style, very different from the light rhythmic tap that I had learnt at Arts Ed. This was a dirty down-to-earth tap, and felt more like stamping in time with the music very loudly. It was hard going on the knees and ankles.

It was at this point that my guardian angel decided to lend a helping hand. Tap has never been my strongest dance style, I was more of a very good faker.

As my friend Sidi Scott would say "Smile and they won't look at your feet." In other words 'Tits and Teeth'. I was just about to start the first tap combination when my toe tap just flew off.

"It's ok Scott, you can dance in your normal shoes." YES. Thank you God. We danced several different combinations and after about two hours we were sent backstage to get our music together to sing.

Well this was it, do or die. I used to like singing auditions, to me it was just me showing off. After about 30 minutes I was called up to the wings to be ready to follow the next boy. That boy was Philip Gould and what a voice! He sang 'I'll build a stairway to paradise' faultlessly. Shit. I'm not following him.

Plan B. I told the stage manager I needed to go to the loo so the guy behind me took my place. Thank God he couldn't sing in tune to save his life. I followed him and ripped the ceiling off with my version of 'Easy Street', throwing in a Top A.

Now the waiting game.

Thankfully, we didn't have to wait long for the next piece of the fun/torture to resume. After the last boy had sung, we were all called to the stage. We huddled together like sheep waiting to go to the slaughter. Randy Skinner came onto the stage, he was the other choreographer for the show and had also been one of Gower Champion's assistants on Broadway. In his hand he had a list. Did this mean that a decision had been made? We had been auditioning for four hours, but for an American production that's not long.

Randy started with the obligatory 'thank you' speech, and then he split us up into groups. I was the first name called and told to move down stage right, there were three groups, one centre stage, the other down stage left, and mine. I seemed to be on my own for an age until I was joined by Richard Calkin, a great dancer but I had not heard him sing, and Steven Lubman, who was very handsome and a fabulous dancer. I was still confused as I saw people I thought would definitely be in the final list standing in different groups all over the stage.

It was only when I saw Philip Gould joining my group that I could hear my heart beating in my ears. "He has to be in. He is a great dancer and has that voice."

At last we were all separated into the three groups. Karen Baker then came back on stage. She walked over to the group down stage left and said "Thank you that's it for today." Then to the centre group "We would like to see you all again next week." Finally she stood in front of our group. "Congratulations you are in. You start rehearsals 18th of June, the show opens....."

From that moment it all became a bit blurred, I just kept saying to myself "You got it. From being eliminated at the first call, you are now one of the first seven to be booked." At last, the prophecy I had made all those years ago was going to come true. For this part of my story, I have to take you back to New Year's Day in 1975.

Martyn Knight and I had decided to go into the West End to catch a show. We wanted to see *Billy* at Drury Lane, starring Michael Crawford and a very young Elaine Paige. By the time we had bought our tickets, we only had money left for two packets of crisps and a bottle of Coke. It had rained all day and we spent the whole time sheltering in the doorway of the old Moss Brothers shop at the end of New Row. We didn't mind as we were young and over-excited. We got to the theatre in plenty of time and as soon as we were allowed, we rushed to our seats, front row in front of the drums. I remember looking up at the magnificently painted ceiling and saying "I'm going to do a show here one day. I'm going to perform on the Drury Lane stage."

By this time Randy was handing out the information papers and was asking us to just have a look and make sure everything was correct. Phone numbers, agents and addresses.

As the lights came up in the auditorium, I could now put a face to all those voices I had been hearing in the dark. One of the faces happened to be someone I had met a few years before.

Michael Stewart, one of the co-writers of the show, was walking down the stalls to the front of the orchestra pit.

"Hello Michael, remember me?"

"I do" he said "but I can't remember from where. You weren't in that dreadful *Hello Dolly* with Danny La Rue were you?"

"No. I was in *Mack and Mabel* in Nottingham."

"Oh God, that was even worse!"

I said my goodbyes and left.

Call the agent, then home. I called the agent.

"She's left for home. Can I take a message?" NO. Call mum. No answer. NO. Call Linda my sister. No answer. I have to tell someone my news. Anyone! Is no one going to answer the phone?

In desperation, I went over to a woman selling Evening Standards outside Victoria Station.

"I'm going to be in a big West End musical on Drury Lane."

"That's nice. Paper dear?"

Ahhhhhh….

Chapter Ten

That first day at school feeling again

Our little flat in Shepherd's Bush had gone West End mad. Catherine Terry was the first to be cast, I was cast a few days later, and Robin Slater two weeks after that. Martyn had unfortunately been eliminated at the first calls along with me. It was usually a disaster for me when I auditioned with him. Once we were up for panto in Bristol and I was calm and ready while Martyn was a wreck, a complete nervous mess. By the time I went in, I had contracted his nerves and sang like a drain. Martyn went in, pulled it together and got the job! On another occasion, we were auditioning for the original cast of *Cats,* and the open call was held at the Palace Theatre. When we arrived it was pandemonium. Too many dancers and not enough time, they were only seeing fifty that day. Martyn and I were in the last group of ten, and the stage management told us to go away and come back at 2 o'clock, in three hours' time. I don't know whose idea it was, but a glass of port was mentioned. Please note that several glasses of port were never mentioned, but by the time we got back I can assure you that a double pirouette was out of the question. We were both eliminated.

It was the first day of rehearsals. Thank God for my two flatmates being with me, it never gets any easier walking into that room on the first day. Your mind keeps telling you, am I good enough? Can I do it? I needn't have worried as the cast were so young, some had done very little work before and were far more nervous than me. We all bonded very quickly,

Our first week consisted of learning the vocals. The score is high for tenors and it was great for me to have a good old sing, but what we were all really looking forward to was leaving the ballet room and working on that stage, the stage I had dreamed of for so many years.

The first thing I did when we got upstairs, was to walk into the auditorium and find that seat, the seat I had sat in all those years before, when I had seen *Billy* with Martyn. I sat down very slowly, closed my eyes and tilted my head back. When I opened them, I could see that very same painted ceiling.

You made it. You are in a show at Drury Lane. Never give up on a dream.

Not a good day to get the sack

The first thing you think when you walk onto the empty stage at Drury Lane, is that it is massive. I had been on the stage many times before at auditions, but when you see it void of any scenery or cloths it is quite breath-taking. Karen and Randy called us to order and rehearsals started. At the front was a line of rehearsal mirrors masking the auditorium from view, and every step was 'cleaned' as we went.

"No, your arm is like this. Your head must tilt like this." We seemed to dance for days in front of that mirror, repeating the same steps over and over until one morning the mirrors had gone. As any dancer will tell you, you think you know the number until you face away from the mirror, then it is all strange. The mirror became your friend, but then you are on your own.

I think we must have rehearsed in practically every theatre in the West End, as we kept moving around like tap dancing gypsies. I do remember that we spent a few days at the Adelphi and we all got flea bites from the dressing room carpet. The reason we couldn't use Drury Lane was because the set had arrived and lights were being rigged. After our mini tour of Shaftesbury Avenue, The Strand and even London Bridge, we came home like excited children returning from a trip. There were newly decorated dressing rooms, new shower rooms and new front of house curtains. David Merrick, the show's producer, had seen the theatre's beautiful red house tabs in a photo and, because of a trick of the light they appeared green, not a lucky colour in the theatre. Mr Merrick had a new pair made.

On the first day back we had another surprise, the orchestra. We were all sitting in the stalls when completely out of the blue they started playing the overture. Slowly we all moved towards the pit, being drawn to the music as if it was calling us. I leant my hands on the pit rail, you could feel the vibrations of all the brass playing and the heartbeat of the drums, in your hands. By the end, we were all clapping and cheering.

The dreaded technical rehearsals started. Why dreaded? Lots of standing around, lots of waiting and lots of doing nothing. The rehearsals so far had been so intense and now we seemed to have stopped. Of course we hadn't, as tech rehearsals are for the crew. I had so many costume changes, and boy do I hate changing costumes, that I was concerned that I would miss one and therefore very keen to rehearse them. The day of the final full tech run arrived, we still hadn't run the whole show in one, and that night was the first preview. We started and it was all going well, then we got to the section where I had four quick changes in a row. We had just finished the 'Dames' number, and I was rushing off for the second quick change when a voice from the dark shouted.

"That's it folks, we have to stop there as the musicians need to have a break before tonight." I was not a happy bunny and went upstairs.

"Well that's it. What will be, will be." It had been one hell of a journey to get here and now it was time to see if all those pieces fitted together.

Only a few weeks earlier, I had thought I was going to get the sack. It had been the day of the press launch, and we were all dressed up in our smart casual clothes, posing for photos and drinking bubbles, when all of a sudden the rumours went round one of the boys had been let go. Who was it? We looked round and noticed that Colin was the only boy missing, so it must have been him. While we were discussing this, I had a tap on my shoulder. It was Roger the stage manager.

"You need to go to the company office after the launch has finished." Oh dear Lord. They were going to sack me! What had I done?

As soon as we were told we had finished for lunch, I went to the office.

"Come in Scott." In the small office was Randy, Karen, and Lucia Victor, the director. "So I guess you've heard the news about Colin?" I gulped. "Well, this affects you also." Here it comes... "We want you to take over Colin's bits as well as doing your own. Is that ok?" I was so relieved I just burst out laughing. Many years later I saw Colin outside a bar in Gran Canaria. I had always felt bad that we had never been given the chance to say goodbye. He laughed too when I told him my story.

How many Hollywood movie stars have you danced with?

The opening night had finally arrived. August 8th 1984 will always hold a special place in my heart, as will the fabulous theatre that is the Theatre Royal in Drury Lane.

For those of you who have experienced an opening night backstage, be it a local amateur production in a village hall or one of the finest theatres in London's West End, the atmosphere is nothing like anything else in the world. It is a strange mixture of anticipation, nerves and pure joy; a little like that feeling a child has on Christmas Eve. That night, it was as if all my Christmas Eves had come at once. I was about to open in the biggest musical to hit the West End in years. I felt as sick as a dog.

As the curtain rose and the iconic opening number of *42nd Street* started, the audience went crazy. The press described the show as "the mother and father of all musical comedies".

The next few hours just flew by, having thirteen costume changes helped I'm sure. As the finale started, I was standing in the wings in my beautiful burgundy tail suit with top hat in hand. I felt even taller than my usual six foot one height. What a night it had been. I entered upstage left and ran on, meeting the other guys entering from the other side of the vast Drury Lane stage, my heart bursting with pride.

The finale was coming to an end and we were taking our last bow when a spotlight hit the Prince of Wales' Box stage left. Drury Lane is the only West End theatre to have two royal boxes, the Prince's Box and the King's Box stage right. Standing in the Prince of Wales' Box was a small old woman in a pale peach, sparkly dress. Who was she? The whispers spread up and down the, may I say, rather splendidly dressed chorus line.

After a few seconds, a voice topped all the whispers. Steven (Lottie) Lubman said in one of his best clipped theatrical voices, slightly reminiscent of a young Noel Coward. "Darlings, it's fucking Ruby Keeler!"

Oh dear Lord, it was the original star from the 1930s *42nd Street* movie! I had just danced for one of the biggest Hollywood musical theatre stars.

As the curtain fell, there were a lot of self-congratulations, hugs, kissing and prayers to the gods of theatre. "Ok, let's get ready for the best first night party ever. See you all at the Savoy!"

Back in our dressing room on the second floor, the room was full of high camp make-up hurriedly wiped off (and a light day slap applied). Our party had already started. What an evening! Standing ovations and Hollywood royalty.

At that moment, an announcement came over the tannoy. "If anyone would like to meet Miss Keeler, she will be on the stage in five minutes."

I think I was down in four. After a few faltering steps on the concrete stairs of the Lane Theatre, I rushed through the pass door into the, by now, cool atmosphere of the stage area. In this production, the stage had been separated into three distinctive sections. At the rear the 'cage' or costume area, in the centre a dock for scenery, and the front for performing. The house tabs were open, revealing the now empty auditorium. The house lights made it look more like a large ballroom, rather than the grand theatre that this old lady of Covent Garden really is.

Sitting on a stool in the centre of the stage was a small-framed lady with tiny feet and hands, holding a programme from our show.

"Hi Hunny, nice to meet you. What do you do in the show? "

I replied as if talking to an old auntie I had not seen in years. "Oh, I'm just one of the kids in the line."

She smiled. "Then you are an important part of the show." She stood up and took my arm. "You know my favourite step? This one." She started to do a time step. I joined in and we danced together for a few precious seconds. I had just danced with Ruby Keeler!! I asked her to sign my first night party invitation, and she did so with pleasure. I said my thank yous and goodbye, heading off to the Savoy for a very special party.

Unfortunately, I have lost the signed invitation over the years. Note to self: Keep the treasures of today. They are your memories of tomorrow.

A little light shoplifting

The coaches were waiting at the stage door to take us to the Savoy, even though the hotel was only a short walk up The Strand. Everyone was dressed in their finest, it was rather like an overdressed trip to the seaside, with the coach being full of over-aged children.

My date for the night had arrived on time. Nicola Blackman looked as splendid as ever and was in great form. As soon as I saw her, I wondered if she would flash her famous tits in front of the star studded gathering. This was an act she was famous for doing at most parties, or any gathering of two or more people. My favourite time that she did this was when she was in *Little Shop of Horrors* at the Comedy Theatre. I met her in-between shows and we went for something to eat at a small restaurant close to her stage door. We had been sitting in the alcove looking out onto the street, when this old tramp walked past and proceeded to flash us his inadequate private parts, at which point Nicola stood up and flashed her world-famous tits. The poor man went into shock and ran off, while Nicola just carried on eating. That's my girl.

We arrived at the party and everything was just as I had expected it to be, wall-to-wall stars, and a room full of electricity powered by the energy projected by my young fellow cast members. The show was and we were the hit of the year. It felt wonderful.

The management in a moment of madness had decided not to invite any of the crew to the Savoy, so another party was in full swing back in the ballet room at the theatre. After a few hours of rubbing shoulders with the celebrity guests, a lot of whom Nicola had either worked with or knew, we headed back to the Lane, but not before 'The Plan'. I can't remember if it was my idea, Nicola's or the alcohol, a bit of all I think, but we decided that the napkins on the buffet would look lovely in my flat, they were pink and had an S emblem in the centre, "S for Scott". We both started to conceal as many of the bloody things about our person as we could. Down underwear (Thank God for Nicola's big tits), in my socks and any other place we could hide them. All fine until my party pal got greedy...

As we passed the door to the function room, we spied a large potted plant.

"That would look great in your flat." said the alcohol i.e. Miss Blackman. She then proceeded to drag it to the front door, bearing in mind this plant was taller than me! As we rounded the corner, a distinguished older man stood in our path.

"Can I help you madam?" The doorman. My quick-thinking friend came straight back.

"It's my corsage and the pin has dropped out!" No charges were brought, and I still have the napkins.

Bold, very confident or just plain cheeky?

A few days after the highs of opening night, I entered the stage door with my whole being filled with new found confidence. I was working in a theatre I loved and doing a job I adored, what more could I want? Then I spied the stage door notice board.

"Tomorrow afternoon, casting for the first cover for the part of Bert Barry, the following names have been selected to be considered for the role."

I looked down the very short list of two names and mine was not one of them. Shoulders back, chest out, without another thought I walked straight to the company manager's office.

"Hello, I was just wondering if I could be seen for the cover audition tomorrow."

After a lot of "well we don't think you'd be right for it" and other excuses, I finally managed to talk my way into getting seen for the part. As I closed the door behind me, I was amazed at my nerve. Was I bold, very confident or just cheeky? A bit of all three I think. Those two years at Arts Ed gave me so much confidence, we were taught to believe in ourselves, work hard and anything could happen, not like today. I cannot believe the attitude of some of the kids who leave college these days, they think everything is just waiting for them on a silver tray. I was doing panto a few years ago in Guildford, when one of the students who was a dancer in the show, turned round and said to me.

"This is my last time in the chorus, I only want to do parts from now on and no understudying." How the hell do they think they can learn the craft if they don't work for it. Don't get me started on that subject.

Luckily in those days I had a photographic memory, so I learnt the dialogue the following morning and was familiar with the song. The part of Bert is a nice little character, he has some good lines and has a duet with Anytime Annie played by my old mate Carol Ball. I was the last to go in, and as I was already in the show, felt no pressure. When you are doing an audition that's not a bad thing. After we had all finished, we were all called in. I got the part.

Not only did I get the cover, I went on many times and took over the part for six weeks when Hugh Futcher, the original UK Bert, left as his replacement could not start straight away. One of the joys of playing Bert, was my own massive dressing room with a shower, TV and a bed. I do recall one period I went on was when Band Aid was on. It was a very hot day and all the windows were wide open around the back of the theatre. As I lay on the bed in-between shows, I could hear the music echoing round the alleyways and back stairwells. It was a real 'Where were you?' moment.

The other stand-out memory of playing Bert was that I got to play opposite the late, great Maggie Courtney, she was a lady and a half. Definitely old school, tough as nails and as camp as Christmas. After my first performance as Bert, I thought everything had gone splendidly. I got the lines right and in the correct order, and I didn't bump into anyone. After the show, Maggie called me to her dressing room.

"Come in Darling." I bounded in, very pleased with myself. "Close the door. Now, when I talk on stage you look at me, nobody else. That's all, you can go." Oops!! Actually, we got on very well after that, and she thanked me after my first stint on and said she had enjoyed working with me. Maggie was not as kind to one of the other performers she worked with. She hated Georgia Brown and this culminated in a big bust up one day during the Regency scene.

The bitch fight at Drury Lane

It was just another day in *42nd Street* land. I had already done four costume changes and we were into the Regency Hotel scene. When you have been in a show for a while, the show just starts and then like a speeding train it is over in what seems minutes. I used to like this scene as it gave me a chance to see and chat to some of my fellow performers that I would never see otherwise. The way the dressing rooms were allocated, the boy dancers and Carol Ball were stage right, while the girls and the other principals were stage left. If you didn't dance or do a scene with someone, you might not talk to or see them for weeks. It was a bit like working in a rather over-dressed factory. The scene started as normal, Georgia threw the glass of champagne over Abner as usual, and made her exit to go to the top section of the set as she had done many times before. At this point Maggie had a few good one liners and a great exit line. Unfortunately, Georgia was having trouble opening the door to her apartment. Eventually, the door did open with a very loud bang just as Maggie was delivering one of her best lines in the show. The bang killed the line dead. Trouble ahead I thought.

In order not to offend, as my mother will be reading this at some point, I am going to substitute the c word for another c word. Let me set the scene. I was playing the barman, and at one point or another, most people would talk to me during the scene as did Maggie that evening.

At the point when the loud bang had just killed Miss Courtney's line completely, she turned to me, her back to the audience and through gritted teeth said "I'm going to fucking kill her."

Oh goody, fireworks. The scene finished, and Georgia ran down the stairs and grabbed Maggie's arm.

"Sorry love I had to kick the fucking door in, it wouldn't open." Georgia said in her distinctive forty Woodbine a day voice.

Maggie firmly removed Georgia's hand and spat out "I'll bet" as she stormed off.

Georgia was not having her get the last word. She stood there, hands on her hips in her best Nancy stance. "Well, don't fucking believe me then, you fat cow!!" At that moment, I don't know whether it was fate or the sound guy having a laugh, but her mike came up just as she said "cow" and the word rattled around the stage. They never really talked again. I loved it.

Sitting in the dark with the king of Broadway

When I first met Mr Merrick, my initial impression of him was that he was a very frail old man. True he had suffered a stroke and walked with a cane or a helping arm to lean on, but if you looked in his eyes you could still see the fire that made him one of the most, if not the most successful producer on Broadway. He was the man who gave the Great White Way *Hello Dolly, Oliver, Mack and Mabel* and many more. That fire would often manifest itself in anger, you didn't know what to do when he shouted, as his speech was so impaired that most of the time you could hardly understand him. He would often insist on giving a speech to the cast on his visits, we would all gather around him and when we were dismissed none of us were any the wiser as to what he had said. You notice I referred to him as Mr Merrick. We never called him David.

92

One afternoon I arrived at work early and they were holding auditions for a replacement for one of the girls. She had been dismissed after receiving two fat letters, that is the company had told her to lose weight on two occasions and she hadn't so she was released from her contract. Mr Merrick was not in a good mood. I snuck into the back of the stalls to watch and sat in the dark as girl after girl came on the stage to sing. After about twenty minutes, a short dark haired girl hit her spot centre stage. Mr Merrick had not seen her walk on as he was talking to Helen Montagu his co-producer, but when he looked up he shouted at the top of his voice, for once totally audible. "Too fat".

I spat the cold drink that I was drinking over the chair in front of me. The poor girl sang her song and left, as did I.

A new contract and a new cast

"The mother and father of all musical comedies" was how the UK press had described our little show. We had indeed become a family with Georgia Brown as our lioness mother and the lovely kind James Laurenson as our doting father. However, it was time for our surrogate parents to move on and we were to get new guardians, but who would it be?

Rumours were rife around the backstage corridors. Names such as Vera Lynn, Shirley Bassey and Joan Collins were mentioned for the part of Dorothy, and Bruce Forsyth, Russ Abbott and even Cliff Richard were spoken about for Mr Marsh. It was a complete surprise when Shani Wallis and my old mate Frankie Vaughan were announced as the two new stars of the show. The part of Peggy was to be played by

Barbara King and the new Billy was Philip Gould, both of whom had been the understudies in the first year.

On the first day of cast replacement rehearsals, Frankie saw me across the stage and came bounding over.

"Am I pleased to see you, a familiar face is just what I need."

Stella, his wife, gave me a big hug. "Frank is very nervous, look after him." I looked after him more than a lot of people ever knew.

Frankie had a hard first few days at rehearsals, he was a singer not an actor, and learning lines was not his forte. Also, his nerves got the better of him when confronted with a scene with lots of other actors. After a few days, Lucia Victor called me to the company office.

"Frankie seems to be more relaxed around you, how would you like to work with him one-to-one?"

Every morning I worked with him in the ballet room, playing all the parts and getting his confidence back. Apart from the first time when he had to face the whole cast and froze, he did ok, but I could often see poor Barbara King's eyes willing him to give her the correct cue.

Shani was a dream to work with. In the cast change, Paul Robinson left the show and I had come out of the habit number and was now the shadow waltz solo dancer. Shani hated it when I was on as Bert and couldn't do the dance number with her.

"You can never leave the show as I only get laughs when you do the waltz with me." Strange as it may seem, Maggie

Courtney hated Shani and only ever referred to her as 'that woman'.

The new family had bonded perfectly. Little did I know that it was all about to change.

Chapter Eleven

Ten hours in high heels

Never volunteer for anything! As no one else wanted to do it, Catherine Terry and myself became joint Equity Deps on the show, and one of my jobs was to organise the holiday roster. By the time I'd finished, there was no room left for a break for me, and it wasn't until I had signed for a second contract, that I got a chance to go away. I didn't mind so much, as doing the show had become a way of life and I loved it! Eight shows a week.

Having spent 18 months without a day off in the show, my partner Jean and I finally managed to take a week in the sun. It was my first of many trips to the islands of Gran Canaria. We both had a wonderful time, but it was while on holiday that I realised that there was a world outside *42nd Street*.

"I have to leave the show and get another job, get in a new show." The problem was that I had to get a part first. I was understudy to a main part in the show, and the only way they would let me go would be if I could invoke the 'Betterment Clause', with the offer of a better job. So, on returning to *42nd Street*, the hunt was on for a new show.

The show I really wanted to do was *Chess*, so my agent at Trends Management sorted out an audition for me. Whilst there, I asked about the show *La Cage aux Folles*.

"Oh no darling, there's nothing in that for you dear. I know the show well and it's not for you!" That's odd because for the Christmas of '85, my friend the divine Nicola Blackman, had given me the LP. On the left top of the sleeve was an inscription 'Your next show'. Time to change agent, I thought!

Luckily, I was still friends with Sally Ann, my old agent at Trends. With more luck casting was being organised by the office above, and I had already worked with one of the guys working on the casting, on *Annie*. After a short meeting, Sally Ann had sorted out an audition for me in the following week, in the final weeks of casting.

Back at work, I cornered my dressing room buddy and still my great friend, Nicky Andrews better known now as the incredible Betty Legs Diamond, to teach me the audition dance numbers. Nicky had been to several auditions already and was a great help.

I remember my first audition was on the Tuesday. No dancing, I was to sing and maybe read. I was led down to the small bar of the Lyric Theatre on Shaftesbury Avenue. As I walked into the bar, my heart stopped. Sitting behind a small table was the Broadway star and writer of the script for *La Cage*, the one and only Harvey Fierstein. I could hear my heart pumping in my ears.

"Hi Scott. What are you going to sing for us today?" came this gravelly voice from behind the small table.

"Easy Street from *Annie*." I said, keeping my cool and pretending I wasn't at all star struck.

I sang, then he asked "Can you sing falsetto?"

I replied in my best Streisand *Funny Girl* voice. "Can I sing falsetto!" Call back for Thursday. Bring dance clothes. Sorted!!

The call back was a breeze thanks to Miss Legs Diamond. The third and final call was going to be a week on Sunday at Her Majesty's Theatre. It was an all-day call including an afternoon call in full make-up and wigs (leotards and shoes will also be supplied). I was beyond excited. This was going to call for a lot of organisation!

Before I go any further, I had better tell you a little about *La Cage Aux Folles*. Based on the original play and successful film, the Broadway musical had received rave reviews and was a multi Tony Award winning production. The story line is around two love stories, a young couple Ann and Jean-Michel, and Jean-Michel's parents, George and his long term husband/wife Albin, a famous drag queen who is the star of the cabaret bar La Cage.

At the club they have a line-up of dancers called Les Cagelles. The part I was up for was Chantal, the song bird of Avignon. In New York they had had twelve Cagelles including a character called Mercedes, but that part was to be cut and all scenes and dialogue given to Chantal, making it a much bigger part. The London show would have only ten Cagelles, eight boys and two girls.

Anyone who has had an audition will understand this feeling. First audition, it sounds like a nice job, I would like to do that. Second audition, I really would love this job. Third audition, I would sell my grandparents to get this job.

I decided to go all out to get this contract and so the plan "make sure you stand out" began.

Firstly, a friend, Jimmy Court, gave me a pair of gold shoes. They were too narrow for me, so Jean, bless him, wore them round the house to stretch them for the big day. Secondly, upstairs in the wardrobe for *42nd Street*, they had some spare costumes; one of them being from the first girl on stage from the "Dames" number. Thanks to my friend Bunny, it was now at my disposal. Thirdly, I purchased a gold leotard from Freeds in Saint Martin's Lane. I bought a small waterfall necklace and earrings from a jewellers in Berwick Street. My final weapon for the day was that Tina, one of the wig dressers from the show, was going to be on the make-up and wig team for that Sunday call.

"Don't worry Scott, I'll save you the best wig and the biggest pair of lashes." All I had to do now was pull it all together and get the fucking job!

So the big day had arrived. The calls started at 10 and my call was at 11. If you have never seen *Phantom of the Opera*, then you have probably never seen inside the magnificent Her Majesty's Theatre. Theatres are strange places without an audience, a little like someone sleeping, waiting to wake up. When there is nobody sitting in the stalls you can hear the noises of the place and feel its energy beating inside yourself. Or was it just my stomach gurgling from no breakfast?

We danced and danced until, at around midday, we were sent upstairs to get into wigs and make- up. I headed to Tina who, as promised, had saved a blonde wig and some corkers of caterpillar eyelashes. She immediately got to work transforming me into another person, and another sex.

Overseeing the whole department was a petite man with a quick tongue and a very "don't mess with me, bitch" manner. He was the legendary Broadway make-up and hair designer

Teddy Azar. Teddy had designed such Broadway shows as *Dreamgirls, Follies* and *42nd Street.* As he walked behind my chair, he stopped, looked in the mirror and put both hands on Tina's shoulders. He moved her to one side and said "I'll take it from here". GULP!

After a few minutes of Teddy starting my make-up, I could actually see my face change shape. With a few strokes of his fine brushes he contoured my nose, shaded my jaw line, and enhanced my cheekbones. Any woman will tell you that when you put your lipstick on, it changes your make-up, but in the case of transforming into a different sex, it is the wig. I held the front of the blonde wig and Teddy placed the back of it on the nape of my neck. When I sat up, I saw the new me for the first time.

The room was full of other dancers going through the same metamorphosis. I could hear lots of them saying things like "Oh I look like my mum", or "It's my sister". For me, I just looked completely different; looking back at me was a cross between Jean Harlow and Ruth Ellis. I was beautiful.

At this point, Teddy placed his hands on my shoulders, not in the matter of fact way he had moved Tina out of the way, but a more gentle gesture. We both looked in the mirror for a few seconds then he lowered his lips to my ear and said in a half-whispered voice "Can you sing and dance?"

I replied still staring at this stranger in the mirror. "Yes I can".

"You are a Cagelle."

It was now time to go back down to the stage. We did a quick re-cap on the dances and then we were led to the downstairs bar where a huge buffet had been laid on. I was far too nervous to eat, but I did take some fruit and water, and tried not to look as if I was terrified.

After lunch we went upstairs again and went through what, when looking back, was my favourite part of the day. We had to take part in a kind of beauty pageant; we were asked to parade round, look in an imaginary mirror, and strike a pose. Just as in the Miss World contest, we had to line up, turn to the side, back, side again, then front, after which we had to sing one by one and then dance again. After about three hours, we were told to wait in the wings. We waited and waited, it felt like we had been in heels for ten hours. It transpired that the production team had four of the dancers at the back of the auditorium trying to persuade one of the boys to take the position of swing in the show. Having done the job, I know how difficult it is.

Eventually, we were called back on stage. Anyone who has ever worked for an American company will know they love to do speeches. Everyone got up to make a speech. Everyone!

Scott Salmon the choreographer did a speech, then the lovely Fritz Holt the producer, did a speech, and finally the Broadway legend Arthur Laurents, author of the book *Gypsy* , and a little show called *West Side Story*, did a speech. A long one!! Finally it was time for the list of Cagelles to be read out.

"If my heart beats any faster, I'm going to pass out! Keep calm and have positive thoughts." I kept repeating in my head. Actually, I didn't have long to wait as mine was the first name on the list, but unfortunately the tension was still in the air as Arthur told us we were in the show as Cagelles, but not what character we were to play. It had to be Chantal or the management from *42nd Street* would not release me from my contract.

At the end of Arthur reading out the list, you guessed it, he went into another speech!

"Excuse me". I took advantage of him taking a breath. "Could you tell us what parts we are playing?"

He started to read from the bottom of the list up, with my name last. "...and finally, Scott St Martyn as Chantal".

One of the reasons I like watching programmes like *X Factor*, is that I know how those people feel. That sudden rush of pure joy, for one moment you are the happiest person in the world. It is your time. Should I laugh or cry? I just stood there as yet another speech started, my mind rushing.

"I'm moving from Drury Lane, the theatre I sat in so many years ago and dreamt of performing on that stage. In a few months I will be working The London Palladium, probably the most famous theatre in the world." This was my time and I was determined to enjoy every minute of it.

I had told my agent the following morning that I wanted to tell them at *42nd Street* first, they could handle everything afterwards. I remember arriving at those famous stage doors saying hi to Steve, the stage door man, turning right at the pass door and knocking at the company manager's office. Paul was not on his own, Mark Bramble, one of the writers of *42nd Street*, was sitting with him having a coffee.

"So I hear your leaving." Mark said. Oh, you know then? Paul stood and shook my hand.

"Congratulations. When do you want to leave?" I had already decided I wanted a holiday so I told them the week before I was to start rehearsals in March.

As I left the room, Mark followed me. "You know *La Cage* will never work in London, not now with all this Aids fear. It is also in the wrong theatre."

From that day on, he called me in a friendly way I hope, the Traitor.

The Magic and being part of it.

Have you ever walked into a room of strangers and felt that you had known everyone all your life? That's how I felt on my first day's rehearsals for *La Cage*. I knew I was going on a funfair ride, but which ride would it be? The carousel or the roller coaster? It turned out to be both in the end.

The large rehearsal studios were close to London Bridge Station and very handy for me as I was living in Nunhead, near Peckham Rye Station. The studios were large and cold, one room was to be used for setting the elaborate dance sections and the second was just as big, used for principal work with a small and separate set of offices to be used by the hair and wig department.

On the first day of a new project, to be greeted by people laughing and having fun as you walk into a room is a good way to banish those first day nerves.

"Hello Chantal."

"I'm Hanna." I was embraced by the larger than life Andy Norman. I had seen Andy many years before in *Gypsy* staring Angela Lansbury, and of course I remembered him from the audition. "Sit with me darling, isn't it all fabulous?"

Denis Quilley came over. "Hello Scott, I saw your name on the cast list, good to be working with you again."

"Great, and we get to do a few scenes together." I said to Denis. We then all settled down for the big meet and greet, before reading the script. It was funny, much funnier than when I had read it on my own in the flat back in Barforth Road. By the end of the reading, the show had brought everyone even closer together. Later on, I understood that was the magic that is *La Cage Aux Folles*.

When you're involved in the re-staging of an already award winning production, you may feel a bit confined in what you do with a character, but Arthur Laurents was very encouraging. He was willing to change things and make them better, to make the character yours. During the second week of rehearsals, I was called into the other space to work with Denis and Gary, the guy playing Francis. I should have returned to the other room when I had finished, but I wasn't going to miss the opportunity to watch one of Broadway's greatest directors at work. He and the American star of the show, the adorable and talented George Hearn, manoeuvred round the stage looking at the scene from literally every angle. There was a lot of "let's try this and can I do that?" I watched for a good forty-five minutes until I was called back to the main room. As I left, I was aware that I had just watched two great minds working a piece that they had been doing for year. Maybe no one else would notice, but a new slightly different version of the 'Mascara number' had just been born and I was at the birth.

In the now familiar, freezing cold rehearsals rooms, large hot air fans had been hired to warm the space before rehearsals, in breaks and at lunch. After doing the vocal warm up, I was told to go next door as it was my turn for the make-up tutorial. Teddy and Tina had made quite a little home in the offices next door. As I walked in, on the right-hand side was a mirror and a table with a plethora of make-up carefully arranged in sections for face, eyes and lips. It was explained that Teddy was to make-up half my face and I was to copy and do the other half. Oh goody, I have always liked drawing and painting, this would be fun. I watched very carefully as he now talked me through the make-up that had been designed for Chantal. I was to look sun-kissed with a pouting mouth and a beauty spot.

I found the whole process fascinating, when I had completed the part of my face, Teddy looked in the mirror. "A+ Scott, you got it in one go. Now take your make-up and brushes, practise when you get home, you'll be fine." Back to rehearsals.

This would be the second set of costumes that I would have had made at the world famous Berman's, both designed by the same person, Theoni V Aldredge. A true Broadway legend, she designed *Annie*, *A Chorus Line*, *42nd Street* and many more. I was so excited about meeting her, as she was going to oversee my fittings. Most of the costumes were coming from the LA production, but as every production had a different colour theme for their finale, a new one was being made for me in 'London Lilac'.

I arrived early. As my Dad would say "If you are late, it means you think your time is more important than theirs".

Ray Holland was in the fitting room before me and when he came out, I asked him "What's she like?" He said nothing, but a big smile spread across his face and I entered the room.

To be fair to Miss Aldredge, she had not had a good week. *La Cage* was not the only show she was working on in London, she was also designing the costumes for the new musical *Chess*, and was having trouble with a certain leading lady in the show who had brought in her own clothes to wear in the show as she didn't like the ones designed for her! I think that would put anyone in a bad mood.

I stood in the middle of the room on two books, as I had forgotten to bring my shoes with me. Firstly, I tried on my opening costumes, the sailor taps, the deco pyjamas and finally the opera coat. Miss Aldredge stood in the corner of the room, chain smoking and making comments on the costumes.

"New ribbons for the coat and we need to lengthen the train, these British girls are tall."

At this point, I decided to join in the conversation. "I have worn your costumes before Miss Aldredge. I was in *42nd Street* for twenty two months."

Theoni stopped what she was writing and lit another cigarette. "Stop talking." End of conversation, I knew when I was beaten.

I have always been a sponge when around gifted people, be they fellow actors, directors, or anyone with talent. I love to observe their craft, and it was drilled into me at college to be pleasant and polite to everyone who you meet in the business. You never know when you will meet that person again and they may be the key to whether you get a job or not. A very good lesson to learn in life. She actually was very nice to me at other meetings, she was just having a bad day.

Doing the can-can is difficult enough, now try it in heels and a dress weighing twenty pounds! Looking back, I can understand why Scott Salmon and his assistant Richard Balestrino made us do the can-can so many times. Stamina! Act One is full-on for the Cagelles, and at the end of Act One I was to have three costume changes, can-can, into kick line, and into opera coats. Fine at the best of times but, after the killer can-can, the last thing you wanted to do was change clothes, do a kick line, change clothes again, and sing. During rehearsals, we regarded it as torture for something we had done wrong but no, they were preparing us for this mini-marathon.

So the show was now fully set and we were all itching to get into The Palladium. Your first day in a new theatre is like any moving day, this was going to be our home for who knows how long. I chose my place very carefully (oh, I forgot to mention, I was early that day), next to the shower was a large two seater sofa that would suit me fine. I could spread out and make it my own. I have to confess that I'm not very tidy in the dressing room, but I know where everything is. The five of us in the room were Andy, Lottie, Ray, John, one of the male swings, and myself. All in all, we got on very well, more of that later.

Our neighbours were Brian Glover playing Mr Dindon, a lovely bubbly northern man, who would often come into our room, plonk himself down on the sofa and say "I've cum in fer me Cagelles fix. Make me laugh." I adored him.

The dressing room next to Brian was the outrageous Phyllida Law, mother of Emma Thompson, a true eccentric. Just down the corridor was the wig department headed now by a dear friend Richard Mawbey. I had known Richard for a few years, he was Nicola Blackman's flat mate and more than qualified for the position, having looked after the international female impersonator, Danny La Rue, touring worldwide. In showbiz he is Mr Wigs.

Let's get this show on the road.

Anyone who ever saw the original production of *La Cage* at The Palladium will understand that technical rehearsals for this show took hours if not days. Before we even stepped onto the stage, there were numerous lighting cues, scenery flying in, cloths opening, and all to music. We were required to stand in full costumes, no wigs and make-up for a long time. I don't think anyone really likes tech rehearsals but they are a necessity if you want the show to run smoothly. After we eventually got to the end of the opening sections, it came to my scene in the apartment with Denis. Cue set change, cue lighting, and Go. The underscore was playing, and I started calling out.

"George!!" I was in full swing, but nothing else seemed to be happening so I went for it, the full three act play. I added dialogue, crossed the stage back and forth with the follow spot chasing me from left to right. It felt as if it went on for hours, then suddenly a voice from the dark shouted.

"Stop. It is ok Scott, I guess we now know you can handle it if the set breaks." Arthur was testing me.

After the scene had finished, I would normally have time for a costume change, then be on for a small scene with Denis again but, as this was a tech run, I was sitting around for a long time.

Richard Balestrino came to my room and asked if I could put my make-up on, as they wanted to test the lighting. Sure, I get to play dress-up. I spent the next hour or so becoming Chantal, and when I had finished I went down to the stalls, just as the stage management called break time. Great, what should I do now? Should I take it off and go get something to eat, or stay made up? I decided to take it off, only to be told they would be doing the lighting test after the hour break, so on the lashes went again.

When we started the evening session, I was ready. I sat at the back of the stalls with fellow cast member Shirley Greenwood (Maggie from the TV series *London's Burning*). I was drawn to Shirley immediately because of her very naughty sense of humour, (a gay man trapped in a woman's body). Shirley and her husband Stan, are still very close friends of ours to this day.

After an hour, Vanessa Lee Hicks came to find me. "We've been broken for the day, you can go home." At least I got some make-up practice and had a scream with Shirl.

A week or so later and we were well and truly moved into our room. Dressing Room H had now been renamed Cell Block H after the Australian soap, and our toilet was now the Cagelle Loo. We had arrived.

Have you ever been in drag? At a party or something like that? I have heard some men who have, but who freaked out and become self-conscious. Not if you are a Cagelle. It gave me power. When a six foot four (in heels) Amazon walks into a room, you notice! Of course, you forget you have all this make-up and wig on, but when you talk, people listen. The crew were very much on guard with us at first, but the more we joked with them, the more relaxed they became. Remember, this was 1986, things were very different then, and Aids was all over the red tops but in the end, even the crew became part of the *La Cage* family.

The first part of technical rehearsals had finished, and we were into dress run, and one of the best things, the sitz prob (the sitting rehearsal) i.e. the band call. Upstairs in the Cinderella Bar, the whole cast waited to hear the amazing overture from Jerry Herman's score. As it started, the hairs on the back of my head stood on end, tears filled my eyes, and I squeezed Shirley's hand. At the end, the entire cast stood and we clapped our hands off. Pure Magic.

"What? We have to do the show in front of strangers?" We had been so involved in the show, we had lived it and become it over the past few weeks and months, that it had passed us by that what we needed next was an audience. We needed to remember how we laughed when we first saw the apartment scenes, how we felt at the end of Act One, and the sheer wonderment of *La Cage*. We needed to share this show with the world. We loved it, but would others?

You would think that previews would take away the excitement of opening night but no, they are really just an extension of the rehearsal period. However, at one preview I was determined to make an impression and work my arse off. The Pro's Matinée was a show for the West End performers, including my *42nd Street* family.

By the time I was standing in the wings waiting to go on, I found out from David Grindrod, the company manager, that over fifty had come from my old company at Drury Lane. I had to be good as my mates would be watching my every move. As I waited for my spot to begin, the adrenaline was pumping in my veins. The vamp started from the orchestra and Denis introduced me. I was aware of the cheers from the *42nd Street* gang, but my focus was pulled to front row centre where Gary Lyons, my old pal from the *Mack and Mabel* days was sitting smiling at me. I had to sing a cadenza in falsetto as Chantal "à la grand opera diva". Gary had played Mary Sunshine in the original London production of *Chicago* and he had the most incredible falsetto voice. Shit! No pressure then. As I started to sing, Gary folded his arms in a "Well go on then, show me what you can do" stance. I sang the hell out of the cadenza that afternoon, and at the end of my song Gary applauded louder than anyone else in the auditorium.

During previews we were called in every day for notes and normally a can-can call. On one of the days, we were called to the stalls for notes and Arthur Laurents went through scene by scene with Scott and Richard inserting their notes as and when. At the end of the notes, Arthur said he wanted to bring a performance to our attention.

"There is someone in this company whose performance is so offensive to me that I have to bring it to your attention. Donald Waugh (he was playing Jacob) you are a disgrace to the black community and if you ever call me Sir again I will kick you from one end of this theatre to the other. If it was in my power to sack you I would." You could hear an eyelash flutter it was so quiet.

The production team left and we sat in silence until Andy broke it. "Who's coming for a coffee before make-up time?" Poor Donald never got over that. Andy would often tease him, saying things like "Arthur's in tonight. I've seen him in the rear circle, with a GUN."

So previews were over and it was time for the opening night. What an opening night! The guest list was enormous. Shirley Bassey, Tina Turner, Billy Connolly, all the stars were out that night. I had crap seats allocated for my family, but luckily my friend Steven Metcalfe had applied for so many, he gave me some of his. Backstage, the smell of what seemed like a thousand bouquets wafted up from the stage door all the way down the Donkey Run.

I remember we stood on the stage before curtain and Arthur told us to remember that night.

"There will never be another first night like this." He was so right.

I made a mental picture in my mind as I looked round at my new family and, at that moment, I felt true love for everyone standing in that circle. It's my happy place when I need to escape and go to a very special time in my life.

Chapter Twelve

Living in a madhouse

It didn't take me long to realise that I was now living and working in Bedlam, not the ordinary Bedlam but a fabulous loving and laughing Bedlam. In the safe confines of the Magic Kingdom, through the blessed stage door, turn left, second star to the right and you find yourself in Cell Block H, a land far away ruled by insane Cagelles. We loved it.

With the pressure of the first night lifted, we could now not only have fun on stage, but also off. In the second act, Andy and I had very little to do, as I did not do the masculinity number and Andy was swing for it. We often sat and talked. One night Brian came into our room with a can of Marks and Spencer's gin and tonic.

"Do any of you girls want this? It was a gift and I don't drink gin."

Well, in for a penny... Andy and I shared the tin between us. It wasn't very strong and it took us the whole of the rest of the show to finish it, so the next day I bought two tins and we had that for a few nights until in the end we decided if we were going to do this every night, we should get a bottle of gin and a bottle of tonic. Then the bright idea was born.

"Let's get a bar!" It would be handy for when friends came back after the show and made perfect sense. In those days you could drink and smoke backstage, no health and safety then, and this was the Cagelles' world.

A few days later, Andy drove to Peckham, close to where I had my flat and we picked up a bar that I had found in an old furniture shop. It was bright orange plastic fabric, studded with gold buttons, and a fake marble top with glass panels that lit up. It was hideously perfect and the Cagelle Bar was born. After starting with gin and tonics, in the end we had a fully equipped bar serving every drink you could imagine. You could have a spirit and a mixer of your choice for a pound. It was the centre of many a party, more of that later.

One day as I walked to the station to catch my train to work, I looked in the window of the toy shop I had passed many times previously. In the display were some blue and pink daisy type head bands. I thought they would be perfect for my fellow Cagelles to wear when putting on our make-up, so I went in and bought five. On arriving in the dressing room, I dealt out the head bands to great hilarity from my fellow Cagelles. After only a few days, Steven Lubman (Lottie) who played Phedra, broke his head band, he always was a clumsy klutz. I returned to the toy shop the next day to purchase a replacement. Unfortunately, they had sold out of blue and pink headbands and only had green and pink left, so I took the new head appendage into work. But what to do? How can one be in a different colour headband? So it was then decided by Andy that we should have a competition to see who would be "Head Girl of the dormitory".

The first Head Girl competition was held the following Saturday, a two show day. Bearing in mind we had to be in an hour before the half to get into make-up, the theme of the contest was the tidiest dressing room place. By 11.30, all of us were cleaning our mirrors and tidying make-up. Lottie even bought fresh flowers. It was madness, all this for a plastic headband.

The first contest was judged by Julia Sutton and she chose John Cumberlidge, one of the swings. Julia and he had worked together before in *Underneath the Arches*. Am I sounding bitter? John had dedicated his place to his mother. Dear Lord, how low can you stoop? This was war!

Gradually the contest grew and grew. It became known as "Cagelle of the week". The themes varied every week; cocktails, poetry, wedding hats… It got so popular, we sometimes had to hold the curtain for the second act as a queen had not been selected!

Poor David Grindrod would rush in. "No Cagelle of the week. No Second Act." We should have charged the audience to come back and watch. One of the contest's biggest fans was the lovely John Avery, the theatre manager. He was also insistent that ice be brought to Cell Block H by a steward after each performance. Andy nicknamed him Mr Ovary and every time he came into our room we all fell into a deep curtsey.

Over the next few months, word of the antics backstage at The Palladium became the talk of other West End shows. One day, David Grindrod came to Cell Block H and told us a young independent film maker, Charlotte Metcalfe, wanted to make a short film about our little dysfunctional world.

A short video was made and, hey presto, Channel 4 took up the option to make a thirty minutes programme. If they had been filming during the following few weeks, it would have been made into a whole TV series.

Andy was once again our queen. As queen, Andy made a proclamation that he was to take a husband. The poor victim (sorry, joyous person) who Andy had chosen to be his consort, was an eighteen year old boy Angus, a dresser who had only just joined our merry band. He was very shy, who could blame him in our company, but he was up for a laugh. Not only did we have a contest to prepare for, we now had a royal wedding. The next matinée day Wednesday, this being the Cagelle wedding, we decided to go all out. The only problem being Andy had written the order of service! Lottie and I were bridesmaids in black, Gareth Johns hired a bishop's costume, and Andy wore white. God help us.

Cell Block H was packed. Every member of the cast rammed into the room. Everything was going to plan up to the moment for the wedding ring. Andy wanted to pay homage to Marianne Faithful, so Angus at the allotted time was to slip a Mars bar in between the cheeks of Andy's... ... you get my drift. At the exact point when the Mars bar was to be, well, you know what, the theatre chaplain decided to pay a visit.

I have never seen a dressing room empty so quickly in my life. George and Denis left on hands and knees, passing the man of God. Brian and some others fell out on to the street through the fire exit, leaving Andy, Lottie and me with the rather flustered man. He just looked at what must have looked like a very bizarre collection of oddities, even for us.

116

"Well" he said. "I've been conducting wedding ceremonies for years, and I always knew something was missing."

Two policemen and the crime of the century

The priest was not the only man in uniform paying us visits. We were sitting at our places getting made up, when two tall handsome policemen walked into our room. We went into overdrive, becoming even more outrageous, with conversation dotted with double entendre. I'm sure the word truncheon was mentioned a lot. The strange thing was, the more we teased our helmeted visitors, the more they loved it. Apparently, there was a police barracks in Berwick St and for some reason the backstage area of The Palladium was on their beat.

They were regular visitors for weeks, and at one point one of our policemen was sitting on the sofa when he looked down at a pair of can-can boots and said "So what size are they then?"

Andy gave me one of those "Let's get 'em" looks. We started dressing our life size dolls with boas, high heels and enough jewellery to sink Esther Williams, there is photo evidence! After that day we never saw them again. Methinks they liked it too much!

Another win by Andy as queen. It was getting a bit predictable, but to be fair, Andy and I, and occasionally Lottie, did spend a lot of time preparing for Saturday.

Props were made, photos taken and sometimes entire costumes were constructed. Poor Lottie used to spend a fortune on the contest, but was always just off the mark. By now the contest was open to all the Cagelles, so even more work was required.

On the Wednesday after Andy's last win, the show was proceeding as normal and we had just finished Act One when, as I walked back into Cell Block H, I was greeted with an hysterical Lottie screaming "They've kidnapped Andy! We have no queen, they've kidnapped Andy."

It transpired that the male singers upstairs had hatched a plot, but what a plot! They had managed to get hold of combat uniforms, blacked out their faces, stormed our dressing room and stolen Andy.

I jumped in to action. "First things first, we need a queen. Who is runner-up this week?" The gorgeous Lisa Henson was called down and crowned in a hurried coronation. Now to find Andy.

The second act had started when Buz Butler ran into the room. "I think you had better come and see this."

I went up to stage right where a group of the crew were pointing to the royal box, thankfully not occupied by any Windsors that afternoon. It was occupied by a certain Cagelle queen. Andy was stark naked, standing at the back of the box on the royal chair that had been graced by the Princess Margaret only a few weeks earlier, with the crown round his neck, his arms tied behind his back and his own crown jewels tucked between his legs. As I reached the wings in disbelief, I looked up as Andy mouthed "Help me."

The orchestra, crew even Denis and George could all see what was going on but thankfully none of the audience witnessed the crime of the century, the kidnapping of a Cagelle queen.

The new in-place in town

As soon as you entered the tiny door of the Piano Bar in Brewer Street, your spirits lifted. Through the smoke filled room, heading to the bar where Madam JoJo, the hostess of this historic venue could always be found holding court, you could hardly hear yourself think over the singer in the corner trying to kill a song from the latest West End musical. It was brash and full of old time West End charm, but it was also a place to feel safe in. I felt at home and, on this particular night, I was by the piano, when I heard the news that Paul Raymond was opening a new night club under the piano bar. It was to be called JoJo's, and I had been told that I was on the first night guest list. Paul Raymond or Mr Soho, as he was known, owned practically all of Soho, having built his empire from the profits of his porno clubs and magazines. He was quite a character, a definite one-off.

The decor of the club was a heady mixture of sleaze and chic, a brothel and a palace. The stairwell down to the main salle was painted bright red, the kind of red you would perhaps call 'slut red'. There was gold art-deco type metal framework on the walls, and you could smell cheap sweet perfume wafting up from behind the bar.

The visual array of the bar that greeted you was somewhat overwhelming, the only way you could describe the bar staff or the Barbettes as they were called, was a group of androgynous beauties, a strange half-breed of half female and half creatures of the night Long legs, high heels, no boobs and exquisite make-up. I guessed that was where the smell of sweet perfume was coming from.

When the club originally opened, it was mostly theatre folk and showgirls from the Raymond review bar. I loved it. I don't quite know how it happened, but I was drinking with Paul Raymond, his daughter Debbie, and JoJo, when we got talking about big cabaret bars in Paris. I wanted to know why they never seemed to work in London.

"You could put a great little cabaret in here with dancers and some drag. I'd love to have a go."

At that point, Paul turned to me and said. "Here's my card. My office at 11.30." I had just talked myself into a job.

I arrived, yes you guessed it, early as always. I sat opposite Paul in his enormous office. The meeting only lasted about twenty minutes and by the end I was booked as director and choreographer for the new show Follies Berzerk.

I stood to shake hands. "Thank you Paul." His handshake stiffened.

"It's Mr Raymond now you work for me." I never called him Paul again.

Back at The Palladium I got permission to do the extra work. I found some boys to dance with me and started to put the show together.

In panto in Bournemouth, I remember Aubrey Budd recounting tales of when he worked for Mr Raymond. He had been choreographer and nude dancer at the Revue Bar. I would delight at his storytelling of the acts with names like Suzie Casino, her act was to spin naked on a roulette wheel, or the off-stage announcement of "Taste the delights of the Tropicana with Banana Split." My favourite of his theatrical fables was when he was at a clean-up call for a number consisting of a line of semi-naked girls sitting on barrels that had a phallic object that girls had to blow up with a foot pump. Mr Raymond commented that he wanted "more pussy".

Aubrey then turned and said. "Why don't you just have a dark stage, and have the girls shine a torch on their fannies on every eight counts."

Mr Raymond replied. "Too lavish. Give them a box of matches."

It was hard work juggling *La Cage* and the club, but it was also great fun. In the show with us, was Ziggy Cartier, Ruby Venezuela, Stella Artois and Madam JoJo herself. The show went down a storm and everything was going smoothly until the night Mr Raymond came early with guests. When the show started, the other three dancers and I spent most of the time dancing on the bar.

The Barbettes would wash the bar area with a mixture of coke and water about ten minutes before we went on, to stop us from sliding about.

Unfortunately Mr Raymond liked a clean bar and insisted it was cleaned immediately. The first number was like a Wembley ice show, but Buz Butler and I had it sorted by the second dance routine, we stuck double-sided gaffer tape to the bottom of our shoes.

No one pees when I'm singing

One Sunday Evening we made the trip to the Donmar Theatre to see the fabulous Barbara Cook. I was lucky enough to go with Denis Quilley, George Hearn and a few other friends. They all went backstage after to see her, but I declined. However the next night, I did get to meet the great lady in a very different situation.

In the show at JoJo's, I basically was a dancer, but I did have a song in the second show. That evening, as we were doing one of the numbers, I saw out of the corner of my eye, that the great lady herself had just come in and was placed in the corner near the pass door to the dressing rooms. At first I was filled with excitement closely followed by panic as my song in the second half was "Losing my mind", one of Barbara's songs. SHIT!!!

The time came for me to sing. I posted Buz Butler at the pass door with strict instructions to watch Miss Cook and observe her reactions. I gave my all that night, channelling my best Broadway Diva. After singing, I ran round to ask what her reaction was. She had gone to the loo and missed the whole song!

After I had recovered my broken ego, having missed my opportunity to perform for a Broadway Diva (because of her weak bladder), I decided I was not going to miss my chance to meet a Broadway legend. Having already missed that window a few nights before at the Donmar, Buz and I went over and introduced ourselves after the show, and she was charming. We stayed and chatted for about half an hour. I didn't mention the song as I could now die happy.

A few weeks went by, and we were filming a *Christmas Night of 100 Stars* at The Palladium. It was the second day of camera rehearsals, and the auditorium was full of many stars, dancers and general theatre folk. We were all waiting around for someone, anyone, to tell us what was happening, when all of a sudden the pass door opened and guess who walked in? That's correct, Miss Cook!

The stalls were a buzz. "It's Barbara Cook!" She walked slowly up the aisle and stood in front of me.

"Hello Scott. How are you? Do you mind if I sit here? I don't know anyone." You could hear jaws dropping, and Miss Cook was forgiven for peeing during my song.

Having the show *A Christmas Night of 100 Stars* filmed at our theatre was a great honour. It was filmed early in December 1986 and our show was closed for four nights, so I managed to catch *Phantom of the Opera*, and have a social life. I had been working for nearly three years in the West End, six nights a week.

On the final day of filming, I arrived at the stage door with Andy Norman, when a taxi pulled up next to us and an arm appeared holding a very large, what we think was a vodka or gin and tonic. The glass was followed by the Broadway and West End star Elaine Stritch. During the filming of the show, Miss Stritch had heard about our bar in the dressing room and the fun began. She was not the only star to grace Cell Block H, as that night, Anita Harris, Su Pollard and Sinnitta were among the many who popped in for a tipple. Things did get out of hand at one point, and the stage manager told us we were no longer allowed to sell drinks to the crew; it was fine for the stars to get pissed, but not the crew!

We did two sections in the show that night, the finale of Act One numbers including the can-can, and the 'Best of Times', then the whole cast was to be on stage for the grand finale. As the cast was enormous, the logistics of getting us all on stage must have been a stage management nightmare; we were all lined up in two massive long lines to wait to enter on to the stage. It just happened that our line of highly made-up can-can dancers was positioned exactly facing the London Gospel Choir. I bet there were a lot of very odd prayers said that night.

The show that changed everything

It was only a few weeks after the *Christmas Night of 100 Stars,* that we got our notice, completely out of the blue. We were held on stage after the final call, and David Grindrod and others from the production team told us the news.

I remember feeling numb. "It's a few weeks before Christmas, what the hell is this?" At least they gave us six weeks' notice. The box office went mad after the news got out, not only were we closing, but we had just started cast replacement rehearsals. Our lovely Denis was leaving, and James Smillie was taking over.

The six weeks just flew by, and 31st January was soon upon us. You don't realise how much crap you accumulate in your dressing room, and it took me best part of a week to sort out and pack all my stuff. I didn't drive in those days, so it was numerous dance bags on many bus and tube trips, until my little corner of Cell Block H was clear. I did revisit my Palladium home on two occasions in later years, once when we did the concert of the show in 1989, and then many years later when my friend Steven Metcalfe had made some replica costumes of the show for a front of house exhibition. When I entered the dressing room, my eyes filled with tears, and I was immediately transported back to those mad, happy days in the land of Cagelles.

After the show closed, it was back to the old routine of auditions, or so I thought. I had not realised that the backlash about *La Cage* would be so harsh; the show had never been nominated for any awards, apart from George for Best Actor. There had even been letters to *The Stage* saying the show promoted promiscuity and was encouraging the gay lifestyle. One letter that we received at the stage door even suggested that if you sat on one of the seats you could catch Aids. I never expected to be discriminated against by my own theatre community.

The first time I was aware of any bad feelings towards the show, was when I was booked in for an audition for a production of *Fiddler on the Roof*. I was up for the Russian suitor, when my agent called and said they had cancelled due to the fact I had been in *La Cage*. The next time was when I had my one and only casting for *Les Miserables* when it was still on at the Palace. I arrived at the theatre, went on stage, sang then waited while the voices in the dark stopped talking about me. After a few minutes, one of the voices said they were going to give me some music to take away and learn, when suddenly I could hear a lot of whispering.

"Scott, were you in *La Cage*?" I told them I was. More whispering. "Thank you Scott. That's all." I left the stage stunned.

I had a meeting with my agent and it was decided that I had to take the show off my CV. It was a sad day for me, not just because I had to sever my connection with a show I loved and of which I was very proud to have been a part, but also that the people I worked with, my own community, had turned against the show just because it had gay connotations.

It was sad to think that after being in this fabulous show for nearly a year, it had turned into the show that changed everything for me, at times not in a good way. It was a bad year for me. I had been working in the West End for three years continuously and, before that, I had rarely been out of work for long. I thought I would never work again, until two very different avenues of work opened up for me.

Chapter Thirteen

Taking two different paths

After waiting for the phone to ring, I decided to go and get my own work.

When *La Cage* was in full swing, I had been invited to be a guest at Roy's Restaurant in the cabaret act of David Raven. Better known as Maisie Trollette, he was at that time one of the UK's leading drag acts, and is still going strong today. I had to ask permission from the management, but they were more than happy as it was good publicity for the show. To my great shock, not only was I a success, but we got another booking. I did a few gigs when the show was still running, then after the show had been given its notice, David called me and asked if I'd like to do a few shows with him after we had finished.

We closed at The Palladium on Saturday, and on the Tuesday I was working at the White Swan in Commercial Road. When the door of the small dressing room closed behind me, I cried, but the money was good and coming from a show like *La Cage*, I was a name and even a star on the gay scene, and I was working.

At the same time, Chrissy Bright, a friend I had met a few years before, called and asked me if I fancied choreographing a show for a local amateur company in Croydon, they were doing *West Side Story*. Within a few months of the show closing, I had become a professional drag queen, and a choreographer on the amateur circuit. How the hell did that happen?

I hated doing the drag shows. It was terrifying. I was used to being in shows that had rehearsals, being on stage with other performers and weeks of perfecting our act together, not improvising everything on the spot. At first I was working with Maisie doing a double, then on a visit to see my friend Nikki Young in Luton, I met the manager of a bar, and he offered me a booking on my own.

Initially I turned it down until Nikki called me to one side. "Listen Pet, take the gig, if you're crap, only twenty queens in Luton will know it." I did the gig and got a few more as a result.

One thing I did notice on my short stint on the crazy ride of the club and pub cabaret world, is that the drag community is, on the whole, a very loyal and supportive group. We were in competition for work for most of the year, but when needed, we worked together. I did numerous charity shows and fundraising functions; these were times I look back on with the fondest memories.

Paul O'Grady, or Lily as we all called him, was a great friend. We worked together many times and everyone knew Paul was destined for better things than the pubs. When I first met him, he was in a mime act called *The Playgirls*. Not many people knew that Paul had a viper-like tongue. I would sit with him some nights and feel ill, I was laughing so much. I have not seen him for years, but I'm sure our paths will cross again one day.

I was still not enjoying doing the shows, but I was paying the bills and earning more money than I had in the West End.

It wasn't until I got together with Steve Metcalfe and we started to put on cabaret shows at the Two Brewers in Clapham, that I started to enjoy the drag. The budgets were generous, and the shows were very lavish, we had boy dancers and a novelty puppet act called 'No Strings'. Steve and I were in the shows, and Maisie was the star. Our first show *Follies Tonite* was a massive success, so successful that we took the show to Brighton. This was the beginning of us taking over the alternative pantos and by the end of the 1980s, the Follies Company ruled the cabaret scene. We were riding high.

At the same time as all the drag shows, I was becoming well established on the amateur scene. I started at Croydon and then Portsmouth. From doing shows at the Kings Theatre in Southsea, I got contracts in Southampton, Weymouth, Yeovil, Frome and St Austell. Later on, I started to work in Wales, the Stoke area, Darlington and the Isle of Man.

By the end of 1987, the phone had started ringing again, and I was back doing what I loved, being in a show.

I was now back on tour again in a show called *S'Wonderful* about the life story of George Gershwin. Another cast reunion for me with Peter Sutherland from *Farewell to the Good Old Days* for the BBC, Marc Urquhart, with whom I shared a dressing room in *Mack and Mabel*, Susannah Fellows from *Me and My Girl* when I was down the road at Drury Lane and, much to my delight, I was again working with Nicola. The director, Chris Masters and choreographer, Christopher Wren, obviously didn't know about our history together and foolishly put us together in lots of the numbers.

At one point, we were doing some obscure Gershwin opera number where I had to die in Nicola's arms. She nearly killed me anyway, as she would insist on pressing me into her ample breasts nightly. We also had to do a dance number together, 'I got Rhythm'. Nicola had to sing a section, do a tap break and then jump off a rostrum onto the main performing area. Then I did the same, but after one rehearsal when she jumped and farted at the same time, we were a mess. Afterwards, every time we got to that part in the show, it was a danger point.

Towards the end of the run, Nicola was going into panto so she had to find a replacement for the last dates in Jersey. She asked me to teach the 'new girl', who just happened to be a certain Rosie Ashe. Oh why did I tell her the farting story? Miss Ashe is queen of gigglers! The tour finished, and I went back to drag, but not for long.

The brighter side of drag

When talking about the brighter side of drag, I should say the Bright side of drag, meaning Chrissy Bright who was my PA and dresser in my short career on the drag circuit. The poor woman drove me up and down the country, sharing the smallest dressing cupboards in the world. Bless her, she would do anything for anyone, but how she has managed to get through life is a miracle.

Her mishaps and faux-pas are now part of folk tales too numerous to share today, but I knew I was in for a fun ride when on one of my first shows, working to backing tracks, she pushed the rewind button instead of the pause one.

I had done a medley from *Hello Dolly* followed by a short warm-up peppered with theatrical anecdotes. I introduced the second number from *42nd Street*, the music started and I had to do the whole of the Dolly section again to a confused audience. I was glaring at Chrissy, but she just smiled back at me, unaware of her mistake.

I had bookings in London, but mainly in Brighton, and when I was down by the coast, I met John Nathan Turner of Dr Who fame, and his partner Gary Downie, an ex Danny La Rue dancer. They were producing a TV programme on the lines of the seventies show *The Comedians*, called *Dragons Live*. It was to feature all the top acts of the day with two, twenty minute spots to be recorded live at the Pavilion Theatre. Much to my surprise, they asked me to do it. I was surprised, because I was not a comic, my act consisted of me singing and telling stories about backstage life, not telling jokes. I came up with a plan, Chrissy was to sit in the front row with every joke I had ever heard written on large idiot cards.

The first half started. I was second on in the first show and second to last in the second, we had to do twenty minutes, not a minute less. My main concern was that I wouldn't have enough material to fill the time. Dave Lynn was on just before me and as he finished his spot, a voice on a microphone came from the back of the auditorium.

"Mr Lynn, could you come back on stage please, you have not done your twenty minutes." I felt sick. I walked on stage faking confidence, but the first joke went down well. Then I got brain freeze and couldn't remember a single joke, so I went into Plan B. Chrissy was sitting front centre next to Tony Page, a well-established drag queen.

———

I looked at her and nodded, waiting for her to turn the card, but to my horror she nodded back! I just roared with laughter. I explained to the audience and they laughed along with me. Out of the fifteen jokes I had on the cards, I only did five and was taken off after twenty five minutes.

My favourite 'Chrissyism' happened a few years later when my talented friend David Dale, had written a play called *Pink for a Boy*, to be performed at the Oldham Coliseum. He offered me the part of Colin aka Mme Fifi, the owner of a drag club. The play was set in the dressing room, but also showed numbers from the cabaret show. At one point I was to play Marilyn in the famous white dress and wind machine section played behind a gauze. I was asked to supply a wig for the scene, and as I didn't have one, I asked Chrissy. She said she did and would bring it over that night. She arrived and I took the plastic bag containing the afore-mentioned wig and put it upstairs with her coat on the bed. Later on in the evening, I popped into the bedroom to have a look and see if it fitted me. I opened the bag to find a pale mousy brown wig!

"Chrissy, what's this wig?" I called down the stairs.

"It's my Monroe wig." I looked at myself in the mirror.

"But Chrissy, Marilyn had peroxide blonde hair."

As quick as a flash, she replied. "It's before she dyed her hair!"

My close personal friends

Before I start this story, I have to say I have the utmost respect and admiration for this person, both his talent and the longevity of his career. However, anyone who truly knew this person knew he could be both devil and saint.

Danny La Rue was at the height of his stardom the highest paid entertainer in the UK but, when with Dan socially, you never knew which Danny, the nice kind, over generous and charming Dan, or the vile, nasty and bad-tempered Dan.

In late February of 1988, Steve Metcalfe, his partner Allan, Chrissy and I, went to carnival in Gran Canaria. Dan was there with John, a friend of his from the old *Soldiers in Skirts* days, and Bruce, who runs a beautiful antique shop in Windsor. One evening Dan invited us all out for a meal in a small restaurant in the Kasbah centre.

"Now, I'm paying for everything tonight, sit where you like. Scott, you sit opposite me." Oh God, I thought, I'm going to have to be on my best behaviour. "What do you want to drink, Scott?" It was going to be a long night, and I didn't want to get pissed.

"I'll just have mineral water please." Dan gave me a look.

"What? Are you not mature enough to have a drink and hold a conversation?" Here we go, I thought.

"I'll have a gin and tonic thank you." If it was going to be a bumpy night, I may as well be well-oiled. Actually, the restaurant was lovely. Dan held court and told numerous tales of stars and celebrities, all of whom seemed to be 'my close personal friends'.

We left the Kasbah and moved on to the Mykonos Bar in the Yumbo Centre, and Dan went on to brandy.

"And not any of that Spanish crap." he barked at the waiter.

A few drinks later and the bar was closing, but Dan hadn't finished. In the end the poor barman had to literally prise the glass from his hand. "How fucking dare you. Do you know who I am? I'm a personal friend of the King of Spain. I could buy this fucking island."

The night was not over yet, we moved over to the Metropol Bar. Dan then decided to tell us all about class. "You see, I was born with class, but Bruce here has no class, he runs a little bric-a-brac shop in Windsor."

At this point, I snapped. Bruce is a kind, sweet person who would never say a bad word about anyone. "Class! Is class telling everyone how much you paid for your hotel and flight, and how much you've paid for this evening? I think Bruce has far more class than you."

Dan went puce. "How dare you? You chorus boy." By this time, we were screaming at each other.

"I may be a chorus boy, Mr La Rue, but I'm a West End chorus boy." Dan stormed off. He went down the stairs and a bee stung him in the eye.

The next day we all received a message. "What a camp night. Let's do it again soon." A few months later, I was in the theatre with my friend Tracy Davenport, and a group of friends from Brighton, seeing Danny in one of his touring shows.

He knew I was in the audience, and mentioned me constantly throughout the show. The only problem was, he got my name wrong.

"I bet Scott St James can't do that." or "I was telling my mate, Scott St James..." The reason for his mistake? One of his ex-dancers Peter St James was my friend from the *Annie* tour, we are both tall and blonde. Dan just blended us together to make one person.

At the end of the show, an usher tapped me on the shoulder. "Mr St James, Mr La Rue would like you to go to his dressing room for drinks." All had been forgiven and forgotten, as it should be.

For the past ten years or so, Steve and I have been touring around pride events collecting money for local charities. I often wear some of Danny's jewellery, costumes and wigs. The general public are always interested in the history of what I'm wearing, it's our way of keeping Dan in the minds of the people who adored him in his lifetime. It is what we call 'keeping the legend alive'.

I know Dan is looking down on us and smiling, telling the nearest angel "Those are my mates, Steve and Scott St James. They're my close personal friends."

R.I.P. Dan. A true star.

Chapter Fourteen

Opium and lesbian sex

It is always a nice surprise on the first day of rehearsals when you see a familiar face. Gary Shail and I go back a long way, we were both at Arts Ed at the same time, and we continued our usual banter as if we had seen each other just the day before. Gary is probably best known for the part of Spider in the film *Quadrophenia,* or from the children's programme *Metal Micky.* He is a down-to-earth, regular kind of guy, great fun and a true friend.

We were now working together on a production of *Poppy,* a musical about the Opium Wars at the Half Moon Theatre in Tower Hamlets. I had some history with the show, having auditioned for the original production a few years before. Also in the show was Josie Lawrence and a young actress called Siobhan Finneran, who is probably better known now from her many TV roles including *Happy Valley, The Loch* and as Miss O'Brian in *Downton Abbey.* Another young actor was Ayub Khan-Din who wrote the very successful film *East is East.* It was a nice, small company and we all pitched in, as it was very much an ensemble piece. I took it upon myself to take two of the younger cast members under my wing, Jon Osbaldeston and Michael Strassen, a young man who I'm sure one day will be one of the UK's top theatre directors. I was a real mother hen with them, teaching them how to prepare their props and costumes before the show, and giving advice on most things theatrical. They were my show babies.

During the rehearsals period, Gary was getting married and I was invited to the stag night. Having never been to one before, strange as that may sound, I was intrigued to find out what it would be like. I arrived with great trepidation and within an hour I decided a lot of alcohol needed to be consumed if I was going to survive the evening. Looking around, I felt as if I was on the set of some East End gangster movie. True, a lot of them were actors, but it certainly wasn't like any party I had been to before. One thing for sure, I felt like 'the only gay in the village'.

I sat in the corner with Stewart Mackintosh, our musical director from the show, and tried to join in the hyper-butch conversations going on around us. An announcement came over the speakers.

"Take your seats gentleman, it's cabaret time." Thank God, a distraction. Maybe a singer, a comic or a band... To my horror, the cabaret started. Strippers! To be honest, a better show was going on around me. By now, most of the guests were drunk, and as soon as the girls started to do their acts, the guys became zombies, drooling and making complete tossers of themselves. It was very funny.

At the end of the so-called show, one of Gary's friends got up on stage.

"Right you lot, I've had a word with the girls and if we collect £50 they will do a lesbian show for us." Oh joy. Gary and some of his friends went round with pint glasses collecting coins and notes. Gary stood in front of me shaking the glass.

"Gary, do you honestly think I'm giving money to see a lesbian sex show?" One of the guys jumped on stage and grabbed the mic. "Come on you wankers, get your money out. If the guy next to you hasn't given, he's a fucking queer." I gave five pounds.

Thankfully, the wedding was a completely different affair. In fact, I would go as far to say it was the best wedding I have ever been to.

Chapter Fifteen

Metropaflop

As I sit down to write this section, I'm smiling to myself. Not because of the great times I had on this production, and I did have some great times doing Metropolis, but because I'm wondering if anyone will believe what went on.

The shows around that season were *Miss Saigon, Aspects of Love and Metropolis*. I'm not really marine material and I didn't fancy *Aspects*. I had heard the demo tapes for *Metropolis* and knew it would run for six weeks, leaving me free to audition for new shows. I was aware of *Metropolis* because when I was in *Poppy*, my friend Petra Siniawski, the choreographer of the show, invited her best mate Peter Walker, who had been the director of the *Annie* tour, to see the show. We chatted and he told me he was going to be assistant director on a new show going into the Piccadilly Theatre - *Metropolis*.

The day of my audition came. I don't know if it was a sign of things to come, but I had very little voice, and what I had was in my boots.

As I walked on stage, I was greeted with "Hello Treasure, how are you my darling?" It was my old friend David Firman, who had been the musical director on *La Cage*. I explained about my vocal situation, or the lack of it.

"It's ok darling, I know what you can do. Sing a few bars and that will be fine." On to the recalls, where I met the outrageous and totally divine Tom Jobe. Tom had played the Arbiter in the original production of *Chess*. We were all told to bring shorts to wear at the audition. I didn't have any, so I went up to Tom and told him I was sorry.

"That's ok hunny, I know who you are, I've seen your legs before." He drawled in his soft American accent. He bent down and whispered in my ear. "You're a Cagelle."

I was booked and, to my great delight, so was Martyn. The first day of rehearsals came, and we met our famous French director, Jerome Savary, a man who spoke very little English. We all sat transfixed as he talked for the first hour. To this day I still don't know what he said. Next we met the writer of the script, Dusty Hughes.

It didn't bode well with his closing remark of "We have the first act for you, you will get the second act when we've finished it."

A woman called Brenda got up and told someone in stage management that she was going. She had won some talent competition and been promised a part, a part that had now been cut.

After lunch, we all settled in for a very long afternoon. We watched the film *Blade Runner* and the original Fritz Lang film. It was during watching the last film I realised that the cast was mostly made up of nut cases. I nearly wet myself from the commentary coming from the row behind me. We had to laugh or we would cry. This was going to be an experience.

One thing we did have, was a good sound. I don't think I had ever worked with such a strong line-up of singers. The score was very high and we were belting out top As like there was no tomorrow. At the end of the first week I thought, if nothing else we sound good. After what seemed months, we moved to the theatre, and then the troubles began. It was the time of the power cuts, some days we sat in the dark for hours. So what did we do? Play chase! The stalls were all covered with dust sheets, so we used to crawl up and down the aisles on our hands and knees.

If we weren't playing, we were eating; Dunkin Donuts was next door. On one occasion, we had been sitting about all mic'd up for what seemed hours when I decided to pop next door and place an order. As I left the stage door they called the cast to the stage and started the scene.

All of a sudden, my voice came over "Two Bavarian cream, two jam and one chocolate." We were never allowed to leave the theatre mic'd up again.

The set was amazing. It consisted of, amongst other things, two enormous trucks that were the machinery rooms under the city. They were worked by hydraulic power, a bit like two massive hovercrafts. The air pumped underneath and you could push them with one hand, bearing in mind one weighed seven tons and the other five. Easy, right? You guessed it. Trouble with a capital T.

The other main problem in the show, was the relationship between Jerome and Brian Blessed. It was one day love, the next hate. Brian called himself the 'Swear Bear', and for good reason. There were children in the show, and the times the chaperones were called to take them away... we lost count. When the arguments started, we just sat around waiting, getting further and further behind. Eventually, the preview date and opening night were put back and we were all on overtime, having to work late nights. The main reason for this was that Jerome loved to talk and the notes' sessions always started late. We knew that if we went over a certain time we would all get extra money, and we took it in turn to ask Jerome a question just at the end, to guarantee he would go over time.

When we did start work, our beloved leader would have ideas and oh, they were the good days. On one such day, he decided we needed more people in a scene, the one where we had a secret meeting with Maria played by the lovely Judy Kuhn. The stage was very dark, and we had miners' lights on our heads, while the children had candles. Jerome decided to have four clothes rails with two dummies on each, wheeled on by certain cast members, me being one of them. Wheeling them on was fine, but as we went off, they couldn't turn round so these odd creatures waddled off backwards, getting a big laugh from cast and crew. They were cut after one day.

Every day we had things cut and added, costumes, scenery and even songs, but the one thing we didn't expect was that they were going to cut the director. The arguments between Brian and Jerome had become so bad that someone had to go. It was not a happy time. Peter Walker was now the director and Brian started rewriting the script. Costumes and songs were put back in, the show had lost control.

The producers hired security guards to stand all day at every entrance, as Jerome had threatened to blow up the theatre. They had orders not to let anyone in with a French accent. The next day, several cast members developed strong Parisian accents, confusing the poor guards but amusing the cast immensely.

The opening night came and the press hated it. Maybe my prediction of a six week run was going to come true but no, the American composer, Joseph Brooks, kept finding money to keep the show going, and the cast kept going too.

One of our favourite games was pass the potato or sometimes tea bag; the thing was not to get caught with it at the end of the scene. To make life even more difficult, on the set we were given goggles with tiny slits to see out. Remembering the set was very high with a gridded floor so you could see the floors below, and we had a very thin bar about waist level to stop us from falling, there were dangers around every corner. At one performance I was turning my cog, when it just came off in my hands. What do I do? I've got to climb down the very unsafe and shaky ladder in a few minutes? So what did I do? I gave it to Martyn. That's what friends are for.

It got to be a regular occurrence that we would go in and be told that a song was cut, or new lyrics were to be learnt. One day you were in a scene, the next out. On one occasion, they called us in to learn a new number for the second act 'This is Life'.

We got the lyrics down and Tom staged it. "Ok, it goes in tonight." The only problem was that Gael, one of the girls, was also filming a commercial and didn't know the new number. "It's ok, just pull her around. She'll be fine."

One of the good things about *Metropolis* was the understudy situation. I was first cover for Marco, and second cover for George and Jeremiah. I got £25 for every solo line I had to sing for any male or female company member. I was often on for Marco, because Robert Fardell, who covered Graham

143

Bickley who played Steven, was always off as he was recording the TV series *Bread*. I sang at least one solo line most nights.

The contract ended after six months and two weeks. *Metropolis* was, at that time, the most expensive musical flop ever.

Chapter Sixteen

The end or just the beginning?

It was during rehearsals for *Metropolis* that I met someone who became very influential in my career. I had been asked to recreate my role of Chantal in the concert version of *La Cage aux Folles,* which was being staged back in its rightful home, The London Palladium, for one night only. It was an amazing evening, a night full of memories. After the performance we all went to the Cinderella Bar for drinks. Seated in the centre of the room holding court was my old sparring partner, Danny La Rue.

As soon as I entered the bar, Dan called me over. "Well done love, sit down and have some champers. You know Barbara Windsor don't you?" I knew of her but I'd never met the living legend that was Miss Windsor before.

"Hello Darling, come here and sit next to me love. This is my husband, Steve." From the first moment we met, "Bar" and I hit it off. We talked about everything, friends we had in common and shows we'd seen. We just clicked. "Here's my phone number. Give us a call and we'll meet up." I took the piece of paper.

Her very cute husband Steve said. "Blimey, she must like you. She never gives out her number to anyone." We did keep in contact and she even came to see *Metropolis*, but it was a few years later that our encounter played a major part in my future.

Christmas 1990 came and went. I was supposed to do panto in Swansea, replacing my friend Leo Andrews as King Neptune, but at the last minute he changed his mind and did the show. Then out of the blue, the show that kept on popping up time after time, surfaced again. Paul Nicholas and David Ian were mounting a concert tour of *Jesus Christ Superstar*, and I was offered the part of Annas again. This was the start of an association with the show for the next few years. We started by doing Sunday nights in Blackpool, the cast consisting mostly of West End performers from different shows.

My tour buddy was a certain young man from the *Miss Saigon* cast called Craig Horwood, now of *Strictly* fame. We had a lot in common, he had been one of Danny's dancers in Australia and he had also done *La Cage* Down Under. We would all meet every Sunday outside the Dominion Theatre in Tottenham Court Road, and travel up by coach.

On one occasion we arrived at the theatre and were doing a sound check, when I looked along the row of seats and said "Has anyone seen Craig?" We had left Craig at the service station about a hundred miles south in skin tight trousers, a leopard print silk bomber jacket and no money. He had to hitch a lift on a coach full of old ladies on a day trip. Luckily, he saw the funny side of it all.

I was back to directing the amateurs again, and doing some cabaret off and on, and much to my delight I was cast to play an Ugly Sister in *Cinderella* in Basildon, working with an old friend, Sarah Payne, a one-time flatmate of Nicola's. I had a ball doing the panto, my fellow sister and I stole the show with rave reviews.

After the panto, it was back to the concert tours and a very special invitation to perform the concert at the Barbican in the presence of Sarah, Duchess of York. Dave Willetts was singing Jesus, Ria Jones as Mary and Chris Biggins as Herod. I embarked on a full tour of *Superstar* with Paul Nicholas playing Jesus for the twenty first anniversary of the show. In total, I did four different cast changes and four contracts of the tour.

By 1993, I was getting so much work on the amateur circuit, I was rehearsing at night and going for castings in the daytime. Something was going to clash eventually, I couldn't have my cake and eat it. I had to make a decision. In one week, I auditioned for the national tour of *Singing in the Rain*, the European tour of *Rocky Horror Show*, and the national tour of *Oklahoma*. I had recalls for all three, and got two of them. It was then that I decided to tell my agent that I was quitting. I told him that I wanted to go while people still wanted me.

As soon as I put the phone down I thought, what have I done? I'm an actor. It is who I am. It is what I am. My main fear was that I would be a nobody. When you meet someone for the first time and they ask "What do you do?" what do I say now? But, within a few months, that decision was out of my hands, and all because of that meeting in the Cinderella Bar at The Palladium.

"Hello is that Scott St Martyn? My name is Kevin Wood, Barbara Windsor thinks you would make a wonderful Ugly Sister. Are you interested?" All thanks to Barbara and Dave Lynn, I was booked to work for Kevin Wood. I worked for him and his family for the next twenty years. Apparently you can have your cake and eat it.

147

Follow the yellow tow rope

One thing that happens when you're directing amateur companies all over the UK, is you clock up a lot of miles. Just for a change, when we had any spare weekends Martyn and I used to drive up and down the country doing theatre workshops. Actually, we had great fun doing it and met some lovely people. On one occasion we were working near Portsmouth doing a one day course and for some reason we both had our cars.

When the time came for us to go home, I said "Follow me Martyn, I know a short cut and the sooner we get home the sooner we can have that G & T in the garden." We got in our cars and all was going well until we hit Balham. My phone rang.

It was Martyn. "Something is wrong with my car, I think the radiator is leaking. Pull over and you'll have to take me to a garage to get some Radweld." I parked up and we found a nearby garage. We bought what we needed and went back to the car. Martyn lifted the bonnet and we both stared into the car's engine hoping, as if by magic, we would know what to do. The top of the radiator came off and the radiator was full of water, so no problem there. We both got back in our cars and drove off.

The phone went again, you've guessed it. Martyn. "You have to pull over, my car is over-heating. You will have to tow me." We parked up, went back to the garage and bought a bright yellow tow rope. When we got back to the car, the first part of the comedy commenced. With me holding one end of the rope and Martyn the other, we both looked at each other

———

thinking "What the hell do we do with this?" Eventually, we managed to tie the rope to each other's cars and drove off.

The phone went. "You're driving too fast, it is very frightening not having control of the car." I started driving more slowly, but Martyn kept putting his foot on the brake. Eventually we got to the traffic lights in Streatham just before you turn onto the South Circular, and I called Martyn.

"Will you stop putting your foot on the brake, I'm going to get whiplash!" I put the phone down and the lights turned green. That was better, and I pulled off much more smoothly. I thought we'll be home for that drink in no time. I looked in the mirror.....no Martyn! I pulled over into the bus stop and saw that tied to the back of my car, on the end of a bright yellow rope, was the best part of the front end of Martyn's car! I stood there for a few minutes scratching my head and then the phone rang.

"I'm at your house. As it was mostly downhill, I just coasted".

I just stood by the road and roared with laughter, not just because half of Martyn's car was attached to mine, but imagining the faces of the other drivers thinking "What is that guy dragging a piece of metal on a yellow rope for?" On arriving home, Martyn was stood in my doorway with two large gin and tonics. The car was a write-off and it cost £25 to have it taken away as scrap.

Three shows a day and my return to musicals

I was still directing full time, but doing panto every year gave me my fix of the performing drug which I still craved.

My first year working for Kevin was like a dream. Barbara had just started in EastEnders, she was with us for the first few days, then had to go off filming. Scott Mitchell, now her husband, was in the show playing Dandini, and Miss Windsor was worried about him.

She said. "Scott love, keep an eye on him will ya, and call me every evening to tell me how everything is going." Barbara liked to be in control and I thought it was sweet that she cared so much for him. Also in the cast was one of the many Blue Peter presenters I would work with over the next twenty years. Mark Curry is from the old school and worked full-out at every rehearsal and show. The management liked me so much they booked me for the following year to play an Ugly Sister again, and to direct the Canterbury production. I was also invited to choose the other Ugly Sister. There was a guy in the amateurs in Portsmouth called Chris Brooke, he was ex-pro having been in *Evita* in town, and *Jesus Christ Superstar* (it's that show again), so I asked him and he agreed to do it.

The star of the show was Martine McCutcheon and she was a dream to work with, a more down to earth person you couldn't hope to meet. Her mother, Jeni and I are still friends today. After Canterbury, we went to High Wycombe to the Swan Theatre and it was there that I first had to go through the torture of three shows a day for the first time. Worse than that, we started at ten in the morning and didn't finish until ten at night. The stars of that show were Gary Wilmott, a very laid back performer, not star-like at all but very chilled, and the tornado that is Bonnie Langford. I knew Bonnie from Arts Ed. She had been in the school when I was in the college. She is in my mind one of the most under-rated musical stars in this country. A true pro.

When the time came for me to be booked for the following year, Kevin said he had a 'maybe' but nothing definite. The maybe turned into a yes and I went to Stevenage, a place that was to be my panto home for the next ten years.

My first *Cinderella* there (I did three in the end) was with another Blue Peter presenter, Romana D'Annunzio, a lovely girl but totally miscast. I always used to say "Can't sing, can't dance, can't act, perfect for panto". Also in the cast, was an up and coming young man called Paul Zerdin, he has just won America's Got Talent and head-lined at Vegas. Before I finished at Stevenage, I was asked to go back the following year. It was to be *Aladdin* with yet another Blue Peter presenter, Diane-Louise Jordan. I get on with most people, but not with her. We clashed, I think it was basically that I wanted to work and she didn't. One joy, was that as the Emperor of China, my beautiful daughter was played by Joanne Ampil who had been Kim in *Miss Saigon*. To hear her sing each night was payment enough. Bliss!

Every year, Stevenage would do a summer musical, using local talent and professional actors. It was after *Aladdin,* that the theatre asked me to direct and choreograph the next production *Hot Mikado,* starring Rusty Lee (love her!). It has always given me great satisfaction to help actors 'get on', so when we were looking to cast the part of KoKo, I suggested my friend Jack Edwards, together with his partner Jacqui to assist me. We formed a partnership and did many shows over many years together; they were truly happy times. *Crazy For You*, *Copacabana*, *West Side Story* and *A Chorus Line,* to name but a few of the shows we did together. On two occasions, I even took parts in them. When fellow director and friend Paul Laidlaw directed *Titanic*, I had the greatest pleasure in playing the part of Thomas Andrews. I shall never forget that feeling of opening the show on my own in the spotlight. A few years later, I played Harold in *The Full Monty*. It's very odd how being naked on stage makes you feel so energised and free. I continued doing panto off and on for the next few years at Stevenage including *Snow White* with my mate Toyah Wilcox; I played her sidekick and we had great fun. I was in *Dick Whittington* with Peter Duncan, another Blue Peter presenter, and another *Cinderella*, where once again, I was able to choose my partner. This was the start of Jack Edwards' association with the Kevin Wood family. Bradley Walsh was the star, and Jack and I were the objects of a lot of his tricks and jokes. He is a naughty boy!

The next year I moved to Guildford to work with Bonnie again, still choreographing at Stevenage. In the following years, I worked with some great people including Lucy Benjamin from EastEnders (I got really drunk at her wedding!) and a trio of amazing women, all amazing for different reasons. Sheila Ferguson of *Three Degrees* fame is a truly inspirational, strong and powerful force of nature. Amanda Barrie, a true legend of British comedy and a person you could talk to about anything, a calm spirit in any situation. Finally, my lovely Lisa Goddard, who is probably the nicest person in the world.

My panto journey was not always that smooth. Back in the early 1980s, Martyn was dancing in panto in Richmond for Lionel Blair. He was also booked to film the *Good Old Days*, when the Panto was extended an extra two weeks and, as he couldn't do the last two Sundays, he asked Lionel if I could stand in for him. I had bought a video camera when on tour in *Annie,* and we had the splendid idea to film Martyn doing the dance numbers, so that I could learn them in my own time. It got to my run-through at the theatre with the cast. The music started, all the dancers all moved to the left and I moved to the right. We had filmed it with me facing him so I had learnt everything the wrong way round. You should have seen the look on Mr Blair's face!

Chapter Seventeen

Living my Dream

Anyone who has never done panto, thinks it is easy to do. It is not! I can't tell you how many people over the years have said things like "Well, you just make it up as you go don't you?" or "It's not like a real show, it is just a lot of mucking about isn't it?"

I did my last two pantos in very large theatres, the New Victoria in Woking, with Joanne Page (Stacey from *Gavin and Stacey*) who was a lovely girl always up for a chat and a great company member, and Michael Aspel, a true gentleman. Every night he would come and find me to say Good Evening. He was an utterly charming man, quiet and always calm. Unfortunately I got pneumonia during the run and was very ill, but still only missed four performances thanks to 'Mr Steroids', the old trooper.

The following year I was at my local Churchill Theatre in Bromley. It was the winter of the heavy snow. I can tell you now that it takes an hour to walk to Bromley from Forest Hill in a foot and a half of snow. That was a walk I won't forget.

The company was great, led by the gorgeous Melinda Messenger, but my heart was not in it. You have to work at such a high energy level in a house that size. I found myself exhausted after every show. Thank God for my dear friend, Jonathan D. Ellis, he kept me going during my flagging moments. We had great many long chats and naughty cakes from Marks and Spencer's.

It was time for a change. As a child, all I had dreamt about was being on stage. I had done things that I never thought I would do, worked with people I had admired for years, been in musicals on stages that Hollywood movie stars had worked on, met most members of the Royal family, and performed in theatres that are household names all over the world. It was more than I had ever dreamt.

One day, I realised I had lived my dream and I didn't have to search for those things any more. I had already done them.

In 2011, Jean my partner of 32 years, and I sold up and moved to a small village just outside Bordeaux. When people ask me what I do now, I say "I'm a West End Wendy".

You see: Once a West End Wendy, always a West End Wendy.

"It's like another language"

A dictionary of theatre terms and phrases

Am Drams - Amateur Dramatics Theatre

Ad Lib – improvised dialogue on stage

Auditorium – where the audience sit and watch the performance

Backstage – part of theatre building behind the stage

Bluebell Girls – World-famous dance troupe based in Paris in the mid-twentieth century

Cadenza – an opera term for a piece of a song

Clean up call – a rehearsal to make sure the show is in good shape

Conduit bar – a metal bar to put in the bottom of a painted cloth to keep it taut

Cue – verbal signal for action

Curtains – at the front of stage. Also called Tab.

Dance captain – in charge of all of the dancers

Donkey Run – a corridor at The London Palladium

Dresser – a crew member who helps the performers get ready for stage

Dress Rehearsal – full costume/lighting/effects/sound action rehearsal

Equity Card – an actor's union card

Equity Deps – union representatives

Flies – area above the stage where flown scenery is kept

Fly – raising scenery above audience sight level

Gauze – a cloth made out of fine fabric which is transparent when lit from behind

Great White Way – Broadway

Green Room – cast/crew recreation room

Hold the curtain – wait to remove the house curtains

House – the audience

Kick line – a line of dancers kicking

Leg – flown cloth or flat, masking side of stage

Library ballet – a dance number in the musical *The Music Man*

Masking – fabric or scenery to stop the audience from seeing into the wings

Milking it - getting the most out of a situation

Off-script – rehearsing without the script

Off stage – outside the performance area

Open calls – an audition open to everyone

Open Dress – a dress rehearsal with an audience

Overture – music which starts a musical performance

Pass Door – door allowing access to the front of house from backstage

Production Singer – a singer who stands in front of dancers in a show, as opposed to a cabaret singer who performs an act alone

Proscenium Arch – the arch framing the stage

Prop – abbreviation for properties, any items used onstage which are not costume or scenery

Radio Mic – personal microphone without power lead

Rake – incline of the stage

Read through – the first reading of the script with full company and director

Red tops – newspapers with a red top, for example *The Sun*

Run through – rehearsal that runs through the show

Show cloth – a cloth with the show's name

Sitz prob – sitting rehearsal in German

Skin Work - performing in animal costumes

Step ball change - a basic dance step

Stalls – seating on the ground floor of auditorium

Tabs – curtain

Tech – Technical Rehearsal

The Stage - theatre magazine with job adverts

Treads – steps or stairs

Truck – a piece of scenery on a platform with wheels

Under dressing – wearing multiple layers of costumes to help quick changes

---

Understudy calls – rehearsals for the understudies

Upstage – the area furthest from audience

UV Act – a variety act working in UV lighting

West End Wendy – a performer, male or female, who works or has worked in the West End

Wardrobe – department for costume

Working an audience – manipulating the audience to react in a certain way

Printed in Great Britain
by Amazon

22207799R10091